4⁰⁰/mup

On the 8·02

On the 8·02

An Informal History of Commuting by Rail in America

Lawrence Grow

A Main Street Press Book
Published by Mayflower Books, Inc., U.S.A. New York

Grand Central Terminal, New York City, Fall, 1940.

Library of Congress Catalog Card Number 79-2791

ISBN 8317-6607-7

Published by Mayflower Books, Inc., U.S.A.
575 Lexington Avenue, New York City 10022

Produced by The Main Street Press, Inc.
42 Main Street, Clinton, New Jersey 08809

Printed in the United States of America

Contents

Foreword

On the 8:02 is the story of the search for suburban Elysian fields during the 19th and early 20th centuries in four major American metropolitan areas—Boston, New York, Philadelphia, and Chicago. It primarily concerns the railroads, the means of reaching out for a new way of life on the part of millions of people during this period, for it was the train, more specifically the commuter train, that defined the extent of these territories and how they were to develop. By no means does the focus on these four cities and their suburbs exhaust the perimeters or possibilities of suburban life. All large cities in America developed a system of rail commutation during the 19th century. Baltimore, Washington, Cleveland, Detroit, Cincinnati, Pittsburgh, Milwaukee, St. Louis, New Orleans—these are among the notable omissions from this book. Even in California, around both Los Angeles and San Francisco, sophisticated suburban rail systems emerged in the late 19th century. A remnant of the Southern Pacific's once-proud fleet of Bay area commuter trains still makes its way through San Mateo County to San Jose. None of these cities, however, developed quite so spectacularly as a center of a universe of commuter rail lines as did the big four of the East and Midwest. And these are the only areas today where service is still extensive.

On the 8:02 addresses itself to the old railroads, the class A carriers that converted to diesel or electric motive power in the 20th century after decades of operating with steam. The rapid transit streetcar and elevated lines, as well as the electric interurbans, are outside the scope of this informal study of the whys and wherefores of traditional suburban railroading. The subject of rapid transit is a chapter in urban transportation history best covered separately, and will be the focus of a second and later volume.

This is a book intended for the general reader and not only for the enjoyment of the rail fan. How trains ran and who operated them is an important matter, but it is well treated in the numerous specialized studies of the various railroad companies. After four introductory chapters devoted to the development of suburbia, a profile of the commuter, the role the railroads played, and the manner and means by which commuting was carried on, the history of major suburban service in each of the four metropolitan areas is explored. Special attention has been given to those lines still existing and to the towns and villages which they serve. The story is that of fifteen railroad companies and their riders over the years. Because the history of the companies themselves is one of almost constant consolidation or merger until the 1900s, numerous smaller, previously independent lines enter into the story. The New Haven system, for instance, was made up of at least 100 leased or directly-owned companies. Now all of the systems in the Northeast are part of the federal Conrail network or are under the jurisdication of regional transportation authorities. In the Chicago area nearly all of the lines are part of the Regional Transportation Authority, and moving stock has been purchased by that public agency. It will not be long before even the names of the historic passenger rail lines are consigned to history. The paths they blazed, however, can serve an even more important role in the urban America of the future. Within several years, the majority of Americans will have developed an economic fondness for the rails.

The writing of any book is a solitary affair. No one but an author can decipher scribbled notes or hastily copied Xeroxes of documents. In putting together a book on railroading, however, the assistance of knowledgeable enthusiasts, scholars, and curators is indispensable. Aid in tracking down dates, corporate decisions and projects, as well as illustrations which give depth to the written record, has been particularly indispensable to assembling *On the 8:02*. Suburban history is largely unrecorded, and its intimate association with the railroads has gone virtually unrecognized. Even the railroads themselves, as the corporate histories testify, make little mention of the development of the commuter passenger business. It is with special appreciation and admiration, then, that the following persons are recognized for their contributions to *On the 8:02:*

John McLeod, Helen M. Rowland, and Ron Shumate of the Association of American Railroads, Washington, D.C.; Marie Spina, Librarian, History Division, Brooklyn Collection, Brooklyn Public Library; Jim Hagle of the Burlington Northern, Chicago; Ranulph Bye, artist, Doylestown, Penn.; Merrie Good, Chase Manhattan Bank Collection, New York City; Thomas J. Judge, Chicago & North Western Transportation Co., Chicago; Norton D. Clark, Newton, Mass.; Vincent Horan, Conrail, Hoboken, N.J.; Ellen Denker, Monmouth County Historical Association, Freehold, N.J.; Jim Scribbins, Milwaukee Road, Chicago; Esther Bromberg, Museum of the City of New York; Earle E. Coleman, University Archivist, Princeton University, Princeton, N.J.; George M. Hart, Railroad Museum of Pennsylvania; Howard F. Greene, Railway & Locomotive Historical Society, Cambridge, Mass.; John White, Curator of Transportation, Smithsonian Institution, Museum of History and Technology, Washington, D.C.; and Thomas T. Taber III, Muncy, Penn.

I. The Search for an Agreeable Society

As long as there have been cities in America, there have been suburbs of them. One, in fact, has continuously confronted and defined the other. Many of the places first chosen as quiet refuges from urban congestion are far from recognizable as peaceful oases today: New York's Harlem and Long Island City, Chicago's academic enclave of Hyde Park, the Roxbury and Brighton sections of Boston, Germantown in Philadelphia. The city swallowed up its suburban villages in the rush to become the metropolis. The flight away from urban sprawl, however, continued further afield—to such now-sooty but historic towns as Jersey City and Elizabeth, New Jersey; White Plains, New York; Cicero, Illinois; Conshohocken, Pennsylvania; Waltham and Quincy, Massachusetts. In the late 19th century, when the city's expanding middle-class population began to break free from city streets—at least during nonworking hours—the search for pastoral fields took on even more complicated geographic and social patterns. Bedroom towns on the perimeter of the city were invaded by the newly prosperous bourgeoisie, and "old money" which had arrived in suburbia earlier fled further into the country: to the North Shores of Boston and Chicago; to Suffolk County, Long Island; to Philadelphia's Main Line; and to the hunt country of central New Jersey. Following both World Wars, vast areas of the last underpopulated tracts within easy traveling distance of the city were fitted with all the perquisites of 20th-century suburban life—sewers, paved and lighted streets, and, most important at the time, garages. And, once again, many of those who had come to suburbia earlier moved on to define a new territory for themselves in what by the mid-'50s was to be termed "exurbia."

For over 140 years, one institution, above all others, has led in shaping the form of suburban life—the railroad. In the late 1830s the New York & Harlem Railroad carried lower Manhattanites to such "hick" villages as Yorkville and Harlem. Out in Jersey by the 1840s, the Morris & Essex had made the Oranges into suburbs of Newark, and a few intrepid souls even ventured forth from these villages to New York each day. These were the earliest of the commuters, and by the end of the century their numbers would be counted in the many hundreds of thousands across the country. During the 19th century, such classic country towns as Stamford, Connecticut, Evanston, Illinois, Wellesley, Massachusetts, and Morristown, New

Jersey, became commuting suburbs. Other communities—such as Garden City, Long Island, Bryn Mawr, Pennsylvania, and Hinsdale, Illinois—were in part the product of the railroad's own industry and venture capital. For what were the railroads in the past but groups of capitalists gathered together to make a profit from transporting freight and passengers? In order to make money, they had to encourage mobility. By harnessing the power of the steam engine, they provided a means of effectively reducing the physical and psychological distance between the city and its future suburbs. It was purely a matter of space and time being conquered by technology.

The moving of freight is a simple matter to understand. But why transport businessmen away from the city and back again the next day? Because, from the 1840s on, it was advantageous to do so. America's major cities had reached a point in their commercial and industrial development which required a plentiful supply of cheap labor and room for manufacturing enterprise. The city, then, was not the kind of environment in which many men of sufficient means wished to live and raise their families. If the early railroad companies had not quite caught on to this desire for greener but accessible pastures in the 1830s, they more than made up for lost time in succeeding years. The railroads were at the right place at the right time. Disgust with political corruption, abhorrence of dirt and clamor, fear of moral corruption and crime, distrust of racial and ethnic minorities, the opportunity to fulfill the American dream of owning one's own home—these were the primary motivating factors which drove more and more prosperous Americans from their native cities to new suburban towns and villages. Most early commuters were businessmen who had to maintain an economic link with the commercial center. Unlike the millions of immigrants who used the city as a way station to reach middle America, the entrepreneur neither needed nor wanted to sever his ties with urban society. He merely wished to place some distance between the pressures of daily life and what he viewed as its deleterious effects, and the comforts and security of home.

Until the post-World War II phenomenon of two-car families and the resultant creation of an efficient network of highways, tunnels, and bridges, the commuter was a railroad man. His daily schedule was determined in large part by the timetable of his suburban line. Just as the railroads in 1883 had established the four American time zones by which clocks have since been set, so, too, had they regulated an important part of the lives of millions of Americans from the mid-19th to the mid-20th centuries. Work for most meant going to the city six days out of the week, Saturday sometimes being only a half-day affair. Not until the 1930s was Saturday service cut back, and this may have been as much a result of the Depression as it was a reflection of a change in work habits and requirements.

The thousands of towns in which commuters settled with their families now total in population more than the cities from which they have been formed. The development was a gradual one in most cases; rarely—until after World War I—were whole new towns created *ex nihilo*. Rather, the territory along the new railroad lines afforded businessmen with a natural and accessible focus for their attention. A majority of the new routes paralleled early turnpikes or well-developed stagecoach lines which had been laid out in paths of least geographic resistance. Although some physical barriers had to be removed, the railroads first followed the natural contours of the landscape, winding around hills and through valleys to reach the small communities where they could unload manufactured goods and the mail and take on agricultural products and outgoing letters and packages. Not until the last decades of the 1800s were some of the rail lines rerouted through tunnels and across viaducts to better approximate the straight line, the shortest distance between two points. By this time, of course, suburbia was well established, and it developed not as one but as many points surrounding the city, each with its coterie of commuters who were accommodated by the railroad companies on what were simply called, until the late 19th century, "accommodation" trains.

Views of Geneva, Illinois, its courthouse and the Fox River, looking northwest, 1900.

Typical of the suburban refuges discovered in the mid-1800s by city businessmen is Geneva, Illinois, a still-quiet town 35 miles west of Chicago in the Fox River Valley. From the 1850s on, when it was reached by the Chicago & North Western, it acquired more and more of the attributes ascribed to what are now termed "bedroom communities." The term, however, is a simplistic one that does little to explain the social development of this town or of the many similar to it. Geneva has been much more than a place to sleep away the effects of work. It was sought out because it appeared to offer a safe harbor for the family. "Many professional men who really belong to Chicago," it was reported in 1879, "have their homes in Geneva, and the society is, therefore, very agreeable." A few pioneer commuters, notably among them railroad company executives, attracted more and more of their own kind. The era of the suburban commuter railroad lasted longer in such distant enclaves than it did in neighborhoods closer to the city. Here still remain not only the transportation facilities which first set the town apart from others, but the social and cultural institutions which reflect the essence of the suburban experience in America, the commuter's passions and prejudices, his hopes and fears. By going back in time to such a community, and tracing its development, one can come closer to an understanding of a way of life which has deep roots in American social and economic history. Geneva, then, can be considered an almost archetypal commuter town.

Chicago & North Western Depot, Geneva, Illinois, 1930s.

Geneva, Illinois, has been known almost since its founding in the mid-1830s as a respectable place in which to live. At one time or another almost every 19th-century American town has been extolled as "salubrious" or "healthful," but Geneva was truly a pleasant site for settlement by New Englanders, both farmers and small entrepreneurs. The gently rolling and wooded landscape contrasted strongly with the somewhat monotonous stretches of plain to the east. It quickly became the county seat of Kane, a distinction which added a professional air to the village and probably no small amount of economic gain. The "Boston Colony" of Congregationalists and Unitarians were among the first to arrive on the scene, and they were joined by their establishment brethren, the Episcopalians. The Unitarian Society's building, the oldest west of the Alleghenies, still stands at the corner of 2nd and James. So, too, do numerous Greek-Revival dwellings erected by early settlers fresh from the village greens of New England and upper New York State. The scene could as well be found in Fairfield, Connecticut, or Hudson, Ohio—each a sober-sided, genteel town of Protestant persuasion which in time would provide a suburban sanctuary from what were perceived as the trials and tribulations of the city.

The railroad did not reach Geneva until 1853, but the lines of communication were already developed between the village and Chicago. The forerunner of the Chicago & North Western, the Galena & Chicago Union Railroad, acquiesced in the request of the town fathers to bring its new westward main line—the Chicago, Dixon & Iowa Air Line Railroad—in their direction. The earlier main route, which passed to the northeast five miles away on a line to Elgin, was gradually replaced as the link to the Mississippi and the territory west of the river. In 1857 Geneva was served by two passenger trains daily. By the late 19th century, the town had become the western terminus of the North Western's Galena Division suburban service, and over thirty daily trains made stops there. It is interesting to note, however, that West Chicago, a more highly industrialized village to the east, was the one to develop as a railroad town. Known earlier as "Junction" or "Turner's Junction," it was originally built up as a connecting point for North Western and for Chicago, Burlington & Quincy trains. The emergence of Geneva as the "end of the line" of suburban service in the last half of the 1800s did not bring with it a shift in the place where trains were maintained. Some suburban trains were kept overnight in readiness for morning runs there, but it was at West Chicago that the "dirty work" was done. Geneva wanted the railroad on its own respectable terms, and in this endeavor was aided immeasurably by two hometown gentlemen—Augustus Herrington, son of the village's founder, who became general solicitor of the North Western, and Ralph C. Richards, his son-in-law, who served as the railroad's

Passenger car built by the Standard Steel Car Co. for the Chicago, Rock Island & Pacific Railroad, 1920s.

general claim agent from 1880 to the 1920s. In a pattern duplicated in select suburban areas across the country during the second half of the 19th century, railroad officials of the Chicago lines encouraged the proper development of the countryside in the vicinity where they themselves lived.

An imposing red brick station of neo-Romanesque design, clearly more monumental than a village of 1,500 people deserved, was opened in Geneva in 1893 and stood undisturbed until the late 1950s. Although the town had developed a small manufacturing base and a growing population of Swedish workers to man the machines, the squirearchy of local professional men and commuting business executives set the tone and the policy of the town. Unlike St. Charles and Elgin to the north and Batavia and Aurora to the south, Geneva was to remain primarily a residential community for the "right sort" of people. When Southern blacks began arriving in the Chicago area in the early 1900s, some settled in these neighboring towns, but not in Geneva. Here they worked only as daily domestics. There was no intention to provide a meaningful place for them in the community, and all attempts

Passenger car built by the Standard Steel Car Co. for the Chicago & North Western Railway, 1920s.

to settle down were firmly turned back. The Republican abolitionist fire of earlier years had cooled considerably.

Sinclair Lewis has well chronicled the "booster" spirit of midwestern towns of this period. Except for the missionary endeavors of the churchly which extended to the heathens of the city and other countries, "improvement" was remarkably community-centered, and was not unlike that found today in Sunbelt areas of America. In Geneva a major campaign was that of beautifying the railroad-station grounds. The Geneva Improvement Association, aided by Richards, had won for the town a station worthy of a Garden City, Long Island, or Bryn Mawr, Pennsylvania. Generations of Garden Club ladies then battled the gritty residue of coal-burning locomotives with petunias and rose bushes. These same zealots supported a first-class public library, a vigorous lecture series, professional music recitals, and a forward-looking community hospital. As even Lewis would admit, not all this flapping about was self-serving or without real cultural merit.

Although a high percentage of the patriarchal residents voted in local, state, and

national elections and vocalized their conservative feelings, most were not terribly interested in what they considered the dirty compromises of politics. Nor were these proper Victorians much concerned about saving the world for democracy; isolationism was an instinctive political response to the growing complexity of the world beyond the village. Many of the early arrivals in town were fleeing the spread of Rum, Romanism, and Rebellion in Chicago, a trend which they both abhored and feared when Irish Catholics began settling in the city in the mid-19th century. After the Great Fire of 1871, when thousands of homes were destroyed and the fear of a recurrence was strong, there was added a more rational reason to move away from the congestion of the city to the country. By the 1890s increasing numbers of prosperous executives saw in the little Fox River Valley community an ideal site for lavish country residences. Soon there would be a country club and a private country day school.

By the 1920s, Geneva was effectively "settled," and would grow little until the post-World War II years. Electric interurban lines linked the town with other towns in the valley and with Chicago, but even this improved accessibility did not markedly effect the town's dimensions or its composition during the first several decades of the 20th century. The situation, of course, was just the opposite in suburban areas such as Evanston and Oak Park which were closely linked to Chicago. There rapid transit lines were competing with the old steam railroads and transporting a lower economic class between bungalow homes and city offices and plants. When the giant interurban system, presided over by financier Samuel Insull, collapsed in the Depression, Geneva's executives were not measurably inconvenienced. Of course some of the businessmen had to absorb a financial loss, but they still had the North Western to rely upon for their daily trip. Closer to the city, a public transportation authority began to assume responsibility for the streetcar and elevated lines which reached out into nearby suburban neighborhoods.

Geneva, because it was less dependent on the disintegrating interurban system than some neighboring towns, became *the* terminus of railroad service in the area during the post-World War II period. Among the loyal riders were members of the Insull family who early found Geneva, in the words of an 1879 Rand McNally travel brochure, "a quiet, restful place, where there is a perpetual air of a New England Sunday afternoon." From the 1930s on, business executives, transferred by their companies from another part of the country to Chicago, discovered that Geneva was a place in which they could lead a life like that enjoyed in Shaker Heights or Port Washington. Generally of a Northern Protestant, middle-class background, they easily blended in with the old Genevans.

If such an old steam-railroad line as the North Western was not to be effectively threatened by the poorly-financed interurban, it was increasingly challenged by the growing use of the automobile and the development of improved state and federal highways. And no wonder. The cutbacks of the Depression years brought the railroad to a state of bankruptcy, and no measure of reorganization could restore its health. By the late 1940s, commuter service to Geneva was a joke. The trains still ran, but the ancient steam locomotives broke down with almost clockwork regularity. The once-shiny steel passenger cars shook and rattled along the ill-kept roadbed. More than once parts fell along the tracks: conductors, throwing open a vestibule's trap door to expose a set of descending steps, watched with horror as the rusted-out stairs collapsed to the platform; signal lanterns were sometimes hurriedly wired to a locomotive which had lost its headlights somewhere en route. Geneva's commuters —and their wives who often watched dinner grow cold—suffered the same indignities

16

and frustrations as suburban families elsewhere at the time. Calling the station for information on arrivals or departures was as futile an exercise as staying clean when perched on a hideously-stained green mohair passenger-car seat.

The Geneva commuters organized to fight railroad management—as suburbanites did in all other territories across the country during the 1940s and '50s. But how could one expect to "win" a contest in which the opponent was already battered? The battle was waged in the courts, in regional, state, and federal hearing rooms before transportation commissions, and, perhaps most importantly, in the legislative bodies where real assistance in the form of public funds could be raised to subsidize hopelessly unprofitable operations. As early as 1908, rail passengers had won the right to hearings and appeals on the fixing of commutation rates, but to force a railroad to continue to run trains without the cash to back up any kind of businesslike operation was a fanciful conceit. Railroads had hardly ever charged commuters more than 2½¢ a mile, and in the 1930s the figure fell to around 1¢. Whether it was known or not, even the broken-down service of the postwar period was a true bargain.

It was something of a miracle that anything could be done to salvage one of the nation's most critical resources. Environmental considerations and fuel cost-effectiveness were hardly thought of at a time when expressways were still being expanded and when automobiles were being increasingly tooled for comfort and speed. An interstate highway did not make its way to Geneva, but there was the East-West Tollway within reach, and some veteran riders of the rails resignedly joined the ranks of two-car families. A management revolution in the North Western system early in the '50s was all that saved the road from losing yet more of its riders and from going on the public dole. President Ben Heineman's moves to modernize the fleet of locomotives and streamline service were extremely effective. By 1956 the whole system was dieselized; in 1959 bi-level gallery cars of the sort first introduced by the Burlington were being pushed to Chicago and pulled back to the suburbs. Eventually the North Western, along with other area commuter lines, would have to turn to a regional authority for financial assistance, but little in the way of trackage and essential service had been sacrificed in the interim. Unfortunately, the same story cannot be told of most of the nation's other commuter lines. Service in many areas was cut by half, if not abandoned altogether.

Geneva did pay, however, for the new efficient approach to railroading: the town lost its imposing station in 1959 to a characterless box, a dreary "shelter" guaranteed to bring tears to the eyes of any railroad fan or aesthetically-sensitive Genevan. It was not surprising that the building should be removed. It was difficult for anyone at the time to justify the high cost of maintaining a high-ceilinged depot fitted with empty passenger and freight rooms and an inadequate plumbing and heating system. Perhaps today the townspeople would rally around this important symbol of their local history and find an adaptive use for it. Twenty years ago, however, the concern was solely with growth, with progress, and new subdivisions were altering the social and economic fabric of the town. At several times in the 1960s and early '70s, even the neo-Romanesque courthouse which has stood in the center of town since 1892 was threatened with demolition. In 1977, however, the building was carefully renovated and put to good use. The "tear-it-down" mob psychology had subsided, hopefully not to gain hold again.

Geneva, nevertheless, has grown ever closer to its big city to the east, just as have, inevitably, other classic country towns over the past century and a half. The quaint and picturesque is now being preserved because it is economically advisable to do so. The price of old homes (what real estate agents once termed "used") is the equal of new buildings. A number of gift shops or boutiques have been established along some of the main streets in what were once gracious residences. Since the 1930s Geneva has been a popular country bazaar for the suburban afluent, and this trend toward specialized shops and services has accelerated greatly. This is, perhaps, the necessary price of maintaining a pleasant townscape. Gift shops with attractive façades are much easier to live with than slick fast-food outlets. But because the town has maintained some sort of environmental equilibrium, and because the railroad is still running and running well, Geneva and the many small communities like it in urban areas of America are even more attractive to those who are now eager to trade unsafe neighborhoods for those where residents are known and trusted, and to exchange cement for grass, rent for mortgage payments, and probably, black for white.

II. The Commuter Species

The commuter has almost always been white, usually Republican, and sometimes snobbish. A good number are certainly prejudiced in that they believe that blacks do not work hard, that they are a shiftless lot who prefer a handout rather than a job. Welfare has never been a particular concern of middle to upper-middle-class enclaves such as Geneva, where it is thought that failure to succeed is the result of a lack of will and intelligence. Sociological portraits of the commuter species are always unflattering, and it is unlikely that they will change appreciably in the future. The pretensions and prejudices of America's Genevas, nevertheless, have been moderated in recent years. Added to the ranks of the junior-executive commuters have been the grandchildren of immigrants, the upwardly mobile of the mid-20th century. Some of the new breed are more royalist than any member of the *ançien régime,* but traditional concepts of ethnic and economic superiority are not voiced with any frequency or conviction. It would be embarrasing and, whether it is realized or not, inconsistent and hypocritical to do so. It is arguable today that suburbia is no more a center of reaction than the working-class neighborhoods from which new commuters have been continually drawn.

The commuter is, then, no easy creature to dissect or to roast. Although there are no statistics to prove the case, it is safe to say that in social attitudes and values today's average daily train rider from any one of the traditional bastions of affluence is at least as progressive a thinker and doer as the majority of his urban brethren. Usually better educated than the average city dweller, he also boasts a higher

Arriving in New York on the Hudson River Railroad, 1860s.

income which at least affords the luxury of some social liberality. While probably not a tradition-bound Democrat, neither is he likely in the 1970s to be of the mossback Republican variety. Eugene McCarthy drew significant support from suburban reformers in 1968, as did Adlai Stevenson, himself a suburbanite, in the 1950s. The anti-Vietnam War movement was fed by a steady stream of cash and moral support from suburban parents and grandparents who, a generation earlier, would never have bucked patriotic duty. The liberal main-line Protestant churches have their greatest strength in suburbia. And, in more recent years, so, too, has Reform Judaism. Sons and daughters of upper-middle-class families have increasingly turned to the professions of college professor, minister, and public administrator or politician. Some sons of successful businessmen have even discovered in the 1970s that there is nothing shameful about working with their hands. Surely there have been and are still critical social problems in suburbia, but there is also strong evidence that the cultural institutions so prized by the more straight-laced reforming ancestors of these modern do-gooders—the well-stocked libraries, the lecture and concert series, quality schools—have contributed immeasurably to the enrichment of American life. The small-town censors were right: a good book can be a subversive thing.

The commuter on any one of the nation's surviving rail lines may be no more tolerant, open-minded, or literate than the one who hops into his car or in a bus each day. Sometimes there is no choice to be made between means of transportation. But strikingly, when there are alternatives to consider, the more thoughtful, albeit old-fashioned, business executive or office worker is likely to opt for the train. The reasons given are not scientifically certifiable, but they do add up to a rational and persuasive argument for many: "I can read or do work on the train more easily"; "We don't have to worry about getting tied up in traffic"; "Bus travel makes me sick to my stomach"; "I like the style of train travel." Increasingly, environmental or economic explanations are marshalled in the defense of railroads. There are other reasons, one suspects, which lie below the surface—a nostalgic liking for the tried-and-true ways of doing things, an idea that train travel is still the only way to go. How else to explain the incredible loyalty of Geneva's North Western commuters during the period when cars were collapsing around them, or, even more pointedly, the persistence of today's determined Long Island Railroad, New Haven, or Jersey Central rider who alternately jokes and weeps over the latest disaster along the line.

Few commuters have been as articulate as Walter Muir Whitehead, the patrician Boston cultural historian. In speaking of the old Andover, Massachusetts, station in the epilogue to *Boston in the Age of John F. Kennedy,* he expresses much of the old-timer's sensibility: "It is a bit of a travesty to speak of the 'Andover station,' for the Boston and Maine Railroad, in its eagerness to discourage passengers, has sold that building to a firm that deals in lawnmowers. There is no ticket office, no proper waiting room; only a crossing-tender with a symbolical red flag, and a platform, left over from better days, from which, on a winter day, one wades through the snow to board the only train. This descent into indecency inspires gloomy reflections each morning…." But, undaunted and resigned, Whitehead adds nonetheless: "I like trains, and regard them as the only rational means for getting in and out of a city. If I am to stick by this conviction and avoid traffic jams, I must now present myself at the Andover station at 7:35 a.m., for there is now no other train." Loyal rail commuters everywhere can only nod their weary heads in agreement.

Historians of American manners and mores probably find the modern fondness for antique forms of transportation somewhat perplexing. Psychiatrists surely ascribe masochistic tendencies to the commuter breed. Even back in the 19th century—the golden age of railroading—the commuter was often an object of derision or abuse. Long Island farmers stoned the first cinder-belching locomotives to come their way in the 1840s; many of the country's most accomplished writers and social critics were just as fierce in their opposition to the dynamo. In response, railroad companies hired such artists as George Innes to wed the train to a pastoral landscape in paintings and engravings; Currier and Ives romanticized the building of the railroad and its service to small towns and cities. The early public-relations agents of the railroad companies were, indeed, quite skillful in their manipulation of public opinion. They published not only brochures and advertisements on scenic vacation spots that could be reached by rail, but, starting in the 1860s, booklets on suburban areas suitable for the city businessman and his family. They knew what they were doing, and what they were doing was to increase substantially their own passenger traffic and, in some cases, to develop profitably lands which the railroads themselves owned.

The railroad was *the* means of escape from the city during the 19th century, and, as the cities became more and more industrialized, the fact that the green countryside was now crisscrossed with rails was viewed more and more positively. Even though railroading was a much more dangerous "sport" at the time than it is today for both rider and employee, the opportunity to inhabit two worlds—urban and suburban—was too good for many to resist. The commuter did not want to become lost in the world, to flee to the wilderness, but rather to put some distance between his business and his pleasure. In this sense, he was by no means a romantic or heroic character, but as John P. Marquand, Christopher Morley, and John Cheever have proved in the 20th century, the commuter is not quite the dullard, the simple-minded boob who chooses only safety and peace of mind over the spice of life. Few of them, in fact, ever measured out their lives in coffee spoons.

What, though, of the wives, so frequently pictured as abandoned in a wasteland without culture? Contrary to the impression given by modern-day social critics, it is unlikely that most wives have felt cut off from life in suburbia. The evidence from Geneva and similar communities in the 19th century is that the work of managing a household, shopping—in the village *and* in the city—and attending to one's cultural obligations was all-encompassing and probably not without some personal profit and pleasure. In fact, it has been argued that the role of women was enhanced in the late 19th century by the very fact that the daytime society in which they moved was "manless." Wives were pushed into or eagerly assumed positions of considerable influence in "improvement" societies concerned with political, economic, and social issues. Although the scope of their activities might be very limited, there is no doubt that the development of such civic groups as the League of Women Voters, the Parent-Teacher Association, and various social reform organizations, including the Urban League, was strongly related to the role played by suburban women. Of the mindless club ladies, rendered so well by Helen Hokinson in *The New Yorker*, there were probably many, but there were also deadly-serious and talented reformers who founded experimental schools, developed innovative health centers, pushed for voting rights, and fought for "culture." Business talents were also developed by suburban women, and from very small beginnings some of the country's largest enterprises have developed in the fields of fashion, food, and giftware.

The children of suburbia have always enjoyed a somewhat privileged place in American society. A move to the country has often been explained as providing the family with a proper environment for education. Suburban parents demanded that their children be given a thorough grounding in basic skills and in the "extras" of music, art, and physical education; many communities could afford to equip a school with a swimming pool and special facilities for art and music instruction. Such institutions as New Trier on Chicago's North Shore and Staples High School in Westport, Connecticut, for example, have been the focus of intense community pride and devotion. Any parent without a serious interest in education was sorely at a loss for conversation in suburbia, where the raising of children has always been the number-one topic. There were also the private schools—country day and boarding academies for boys and for girls. Some children were sent back to the city for special education—to Horace Mann in New York or Germantown Friends in Philadelphia, for example—or farther afield to the green fields of New England and the Middle Atlantic states. In the most affluent suburban communities, an extra measure of education was thought necessary to send a daughter off to one of the Seven Sisters or a son to the Ivy League.

A thorough education, however, could be a dangerous thing in the hands of gifted teachers. Unlike many city ghetto or farm children, the suburban child was likely to see much of the wider world through both books and travel. Trips to the city were natural for the commuter's son or daughter, and, even when strictly chaperoned, the child saw more of how life was led elsewhere than did his rural contemporaries. Many city children, of course, had no opportunity to view cultural differences since they rarely, if ever, traveled. It was not necessary for the suburban child to catch a fast freight to the city; he merely escaped on the regular passenger train—sometimes to summer camp or college, but sometimes for good. He knew that there was a way "out," and most often had the means and manners necessary to survive away from home. The wonder is that so many children of suburbia over the years have chosen to return to their home territory or one like it to raise yet another commuter generation.

Long Island Railroad passenger car with female trainmen, 1943.

If suburban husbands enjoyed a pleasant home life, they also welcomed the time to themselves which traveling back and forth to the city afforded. The train was very much a male bastion where one was free to read, to catch up on paper work, sleep, or daydream. There were always women among the passengers, and their number grew with time, but the atmosphere was decidedly comradely. Apropos of another clubby scene, one writer commented in 1908, "It was like a commuter's train going out to Jersey at 6 o'clock." But just as in a good gentleman's club, privacy was and is respected. Talkers are usually shunned, especially so if they are not known to be one of the regular crowd. Recognition is nearly silent and social rules rarely need enforcing. "Women and children, of course," explained one Long Island commuter, "are the great disrupters of peaceful commutation." Matinee day — Wednesday — in the New York area has been feared by the male regulars ever since the various lines serving the city cut back on their service by eliminating off-hour trains, thus forcing the female theater crowd onto early-morning commuter runs. Exuberant ladies off on a midweek lark are studiously shunned by regulars who burrow even deeper in their daily newspapers to escape the din.

Railroading has always been a particular male interest, and has been traditionally encouraged from childhood with model railroading. Is there an American boy alive today who did not have some form of locomotive and cars to pull around the floor, however primitive or sophisticated? It is hard to conceive of a woman singing "I've Been Working On the Railroad." Only during World War II did women perform any

Cab end of a locomotive and its attachments, New York Central & Hudson River Railroad, 1889.

Among the fixtures are a steam gauge to indicate boiler pressure (5); a pressure gauge for air brake (7); an automatic lubricator for oiling main valves (9); a train bell or gong (3); an engine bell rope (1). Although the engraving dates from the 1880s, the engine is an earlier type.

of the standard jobs of running a commuter line. It sometimes seems that men who once played with model trains have merely substituted the real thing for the toy in their adult daily lives. A recent *New York Times* article on the Long Island Railroad's program of giving commuters a chance to ride in a locomotive cab reports that it has been such a success that the line has had to compile a lengthy waiting list. Railroad fan clubs are almost uniformly male in membership, and their excursions on old steam-powered trains never fail to attract a gung-ho crowd. One would think that the commuting fellows would have traveled enough during the week, but they are among the most fervent of the participants in planned weekend outings along America's railways.

Interest in railroading is also, of course, a reflection of the common experience of traveling from a particular place over a period of time. While similar educational ties, vocations, and avocations supply something of the social cement which binds together groups of commuters, it is the ability to survive with gentlemanly aplomb the daily grind and the not uncommon little mechanical crises which punctuate so much suburban travel, especially in the winter, that marks a man as a regular, dependable acquaintance, and perhaps a friend. Railroading is a crude sort of democracy, a traveling fraternity. Unfortunately, for most of the brotherhood, the good old days are indeed in the past. Economic and social conditions are changing so rapidly in these last decades of the 20th century that there cannot be the familiar continuity of repeated experience and faces. Today the "old guard" on the typical commuter train is likely to be made up of five-year veterans, a good proportion of them businesswomen.

Suburban lines were designed and built to serve the changing, expanding profile of commutation, the gradual filling in of the countryside from the outskirts of the city to the exurban hinterlands. With the use of the automobile in the 20th century to reach distant stations, more and more of the far country — middle Bucks County in Pennsylvania, Connecticut's eastern Fairfield County, the North Shore of Boston — was drawn into closer communication with the city. Man's continuing desire to escape from the pressures, but not the pleasures, of the city by making his permanent home in remote but yet accessible rural villages could then be accommodated in the mid-20th century. By the 1970s, however, it has become increasingly clear that there is little new territory to be conquered along the historic rail lines and that the increasingly high cost of automobile travel will preclude the further extension of suburbia into the yet more distant reaches of exurbia. We have reached the end of the traditional suburban line.

III. "Something Lighter or More Agreeable"

The development of suburban railroad lines is a chapter in American transportation history which has been sorely neglected. Few of the company histories written over the past ten years have devoted more than a few lines to the subject, a surprising omission since urban and economic history have been pursued with new sophistication and energy since the 1960s. For many years, railroads have been written about in terms of long-distance travel, understandably a more romantic and engaging area of study. The *Twentieth Century Limited* will beat the "8:02" in any popularity contest. Speed has always dominated our thinking about travel. The "local," however, has more directly affected our lives than any streamliner streaking between one city and another. Now style also intrigues us, and the pokey commuter train—in many areas the last remnant of passenger service—has a character all its own. Winding its way through slums and decaying factories, alongside historic rivers and valleys, cutting through woods and main streets, the local provides a view of an American landscape which is linked to the past and to the ground, not to an expressway view of time removed from any humanizing roots of the past.

How and when did commuter railroading begin? Precise data on the issue of the first commutation tickets is hard to come by. Just how and when one designates a "passenger" a "commuter" is a similarly "iffy" proposition. "To commute" in the 19th century, as now, was to travel at a special rate, always a rate reduced from that of regular travel. By mid-century, those whose tickets were "commuted" became "commuters," and almost all of them were businessmen who literally struck a bargain with the railroad in exchange for their patronage. If they indeed did "change an obligation, etc., into something lighter or more agreeable," as the dictionary defines the infinitive "to commute," is a matter of interpretation. The early commuters certainly felt they were doing so.

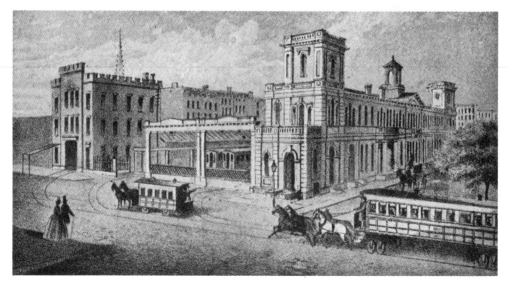

New York & Harlem Railroad Depot, Madison Square, New York City, 1860.

Both Boston and Philadelphia railroads have claimed to have been the first to serve suburban residents. Fragmentary evidence suggests, however, that the historic honors belong to the New York & Harlem Railroad, now the Harlem Division of the old New York Central. As early as 1833 trains were running to Murray Hill. By 1837 passengers were carried to the new residential districts of Yorkville and Harlem. Only the necessity of tunneling through bedrock between

88th and 95th Streets and crossing Harlem creek or marsh between 103rd and 106th Streets prevented earlier completion of the Harlem terminus. This, however, was only a temporary end of the line. The intention was to extend it in the direction of Albany, crossing the countryside as far as Chatham in Columbia County to meet the Western Railroad of Massachusetts' proposed route to Albany. Building along the Hudson shore toward Albany had not been proposed originally because that city and the villages en route were already reached by steamboat service. The Harlem's managers, the historical record suggests, were interested in developing the railroad as a common carrier of both freight and passengers to the northeastern outskirts of the city and as an intercity alternative to steamship travel. It was not long before they were able to develop a good passenger trade seeking to reach and return from the country settlements of upper Manhattan and lower Westchester.

John Stephenson's Harlaem Coach Factory, New York City, c. 1840.

In a pattern followed almost exactly by later railroads, the Harlem invested in real estate along the route and erected, first, a hotel at its Yorkville terminus, and, then, a second in Harlem at 125th Street. These were designed to attract city dwellers to the "country," and trains were run, according to an 1835 account, "for the accommodation of those who desire to get out of the city for a short time." They ran almost every hour of the day. These were the first "accommodation" trains, so-called to differentiate them from express passenger or freight trains. They were scheduled to accommodate the needs of local passengers. At first, a great deal of traveling was done simply for pleasure. Various improvements at Harlem, the *New York Herald* editorialized in 1839, "will make Harlem a fashionable rival to Hoboken, New Brighton, and other summer resorts." But some of the visitors from the city were easily persuaded to extend their stay. Harlem, a 17th-century Dutch village, was in the process of becoming a major residential and manufacturing center. In the 1830s John Stephenson established there his Harlaem Coach Factory for the manufacture of railroad cars and streetcars.

It was not long before such settlements as Mott Haven, Melrose, and Morrisania (all three were originally included in Morrisania township), West Farms, Tremont, and Fordham graduated from rural status to that of suburban respectability. The Harlem reached Fordham by 1841, and by 1848 the line not only extended as far as Croton Falls but was linked up to the New York & New Haven at Mt. Vernon. "The railroad developed Westchester County amazingly," New York Central historian Alvin Harlow has written. "Villages grew like weeds, and a new type of man, the commuter was born." In the late 1840s, the area north of Mott Haven was described as:

> a charmingly rural region; green, grassy lawns, forest-trees, rugged rocks, and the beautifully clear Bronx river, are combined in a series of ever-varying landscapes, in the midst of which are nestled many elegant and commodious villas and cottages, surrounded by walks, drives, and gardens.

It was predicted at the time that lower Westchester (now the Bronx) would eventually be "joined together in one united settlement, forming a continuation of the parent metropolis of New York." Why?

> The enormous rents and taxes of the city are rapidly driving its population to seek homes where these burdens are lighter, and where fresh air, green fields, fruit trees, and pleasant flower-gardens may be added to the comforts of home.

Grand Central Depot, New York City, c. 1880.

Already such settlements as Eastchester, New Rochelle, and Pelham were being identified in railroad travel literature of the late '40s as suburban towns, and the latter two could be reached via the New York & New Haven.

Across the river in New Jersey, two railroads launched in the 1830s—the Paterson & Hudson, later part of the Erie main line, and the Morris & Essex, the future suburban backbone of the Lackawanna—provided commuter service by the '40s to Hoboken, Newark, and Jersey City as well as to New York via East River ferries. Paterson has been an important American railroad town from the 1830s, and it is here that some of the most important early locomotives were produced in the factory of Rogers, Ketchum, and Grosvenor, predecessor to the New Jersey Locomotive Co., and the Grant Locomotive Works. The businessmen of Paterson strongly promoted the transportation link to the southeast by providing in 1843 a special commutation rate. At that time they announced to the public: "Persons wishing to commute for transportation at the present reduced price can enter into such an agreement by calling on an agent of the company." By 1847 it was reported in the press that "Many men carrying on business in New York—merchants and manu-facturers and others—have purchased residences along the line of that rail-road, . . ."

Matthias Halstead, a New York merchant, was the first known commuter on the Morris & Essex. Through default in the early 1840s, rural property in a quiet area between East Orange and Orange became his. After inspecting it, he decided that it would provide an ideal site for a country residence. Soon New York business friends joined him in the building of homes. A depot was built at Halstead's personal expense, a practice copied by other wealthy suburbanites in succeeding years. The station, of course, is long gone. So, too, is the village, but a traveler today on the Morristown line of the Erie-Lackawanna can still alight or depart at the "Brick Church" stop.

The Morris & Essex builders received a state charter in 1835 to lay out a railroad "from Morristown to some point in Essex County contiguous to the tidewater, near the harbor of New York, in such a manner as to facilitate the intercourse between the country and the city." The railroad reached as far as Newark until the 1860s when it was finally given the right to extend its line to the Hoboken docks. Until that time, commuting to and from New York meant linking up with the New Jersey Railroad (made part of the Pennsylvania system in 1871) for a trip to Jersey City. The cars were always crowded, and until the first tunnel was blasted through Bergen Hill outside Jersey City in 1860, there was the dangerous Bergen Cut to negotiate. The New Jersey Railroad and the Paterson & Hudson had cooperated on slicing through the great hill which is part of the southern extension of the Palisades in 1838, and, at the time, they could not have forseen how much traffic would have to be squeezed through the opening within ten years. By 1848 the Paterson line had joined with the Erie, and—with a northern link called the Paterson & Ramapo Railroad—was providing through-line service to the West. Early Jersey commuters had to love the country in order to endure the daily trips. The roadbed of the Morris & Essex, for example, was notoriously infirm and until 1844 was laid with strap rails rather than T-bars which had the unfortunate tendency to break loose and project through the passenger-car floor. One early Morristown commuter, Vincent B. King, recounted later that the "snakeheads" (tips of the protruding rails) so terrified him that he insisted on making the trip standing in the aisle.

Despite the difficulties of travel, the ranks of commuters kept growing wherever there were cities. By the 1840s the schedules of railroads in the Boston and Philadelphia areas reflected the growth of suburbia. The Boston & Maine was serving Malden and Melrose; Newton, Brookline, Needham, and Natick were on the Boston & Worcester (later Boston & Albany); the Old Colony was running frequent trains to South Boston, Quincy, and Braintree. In Philadelphia the Philadelphia, Germantown & Norristown reached as far west as Norristown and provided frequent service to Chestnut Hill and Germantown. Exactly when and to what extent these lines encouraged "commutation" is hard to determine precisely, but there was gradual growth in such passenger traffic as there was from the 1840s on in the New York area. The very pressure of the expanding urban population meant that undeveloped real estate in close proximity to the city would be purchased and subdivided for residential housing. Between 1845 and 1855, for example, the population of the lower half of the Bronx doubled, and all this territory was within reach of the Harlem trains. By the Civil War even Chicago had begun some commuter service, and it was natural that people should have been exploring the territory opened up by railroad lines. They turned first to the open land beside the tracks and to the classic country villages, gradually fanning out in larger and larger circles.

Publicists for the railroads did their best to encourage suburban development. J. K. Hoyt, a resident of Madison, New Jersey, on the Lackawanna's Morris & Essex Division, contributed a stirring promotion piece entitled *Pen and Pencil Pictures on the Delaware, Lackawanna and Western* in 1874. He challenged every thinking man to take part in the planning of "The Coming City":

> New York must remain the metropolis of the Western world....We say [the population] must increase. We should rather say that its suburbs must increase, for New York proper cannot even now begin to contain the people who legitimately belong to it by the force of business gravitation....It is even now the city of the very rich and the very poor, and when we are solemnly told that even a "flat" in a fashionable location brings $6,000 a year, it needs no prophet to tell us of the future on that island of Manhattan.

Shades of yesteryear! How right Mr. Hoyt was. And how earnestly he attempted to persuade New York's businessmen to raise their families along the Lackawanna line. Descriptions of each of the communities were provided, and Hoyt's volume ended with a listing of real estate agents—many with offices in lower Manhattan—who could be counted on for assistance in making the move.

Throughout the final decades of the 19th century, the railroad companies did their best to develop suburbia. Since 1864, the Central Railroad of New Jersey had been able to offer passenger service directly from the Communipaw Ferry terminal at Jersey City to a string of commuter towns beginning with Elizabeth. By 1890 the main suburban territory stretched as far west as Somerville in central Somerset County. At this time, however, the Jersey Central was most interested in building up such readily accessible towns as Bound Brook, Plainfield, and Dunellen. An illustrated guide book by Gustav Kobbé was issued by the railroad in 1881 and included, in addition to the usual booster prose on the merits of each residential stop along the line, information on commutation rates and the costs of buying or renting a house in a particular village or town. Tickets could be bought daily, monthly, every three months, twice a year, or yearly. The cost of a Jersey City-Dunellen round-trip ticket, for instance, was $1.40. On a monthly basis, figuring on an average of 24 round trips (Saturday was still a work day), the daily expense was 46¢.

If one could lay out the cost of a yearly ticket, $90, the price of going back and forth to Jersey City was approximately 30¢. Dunellen was 26 rail miles from Jersey City terminal. Even on a daily basis the cost per mile was little more than 2½¢. The average commuter probably paid something like a penny a mile, a bargain in any era of travel.

Building lots in Dunellen at the time were listed as $200 and up. A "modern house, with all improvements, and desirably located" could be rented there yearly for $150 or more. In nearby Cranford, it was reported, "houses are let as fast as they are built." By 1900, more than 50,000 New Jersey residents were commuting back and forth to New York, and that figure would nearly double in the next twenty years.

In the 1890s New York absorbed as much of its old suburban territory as it could politically and economically. All of Brooklyn, Queens, Staten Island, and the lower Westchester towns newly constituted as the Bronx became the focus of intensive urban development. Some areas remained basically rural in composition and mood until later years, but these were either still too difficult to reach at the turn of the century, not lying close to a well-established rail line, or were not sufficiently attractive for the well-heeled businessman. Even when Forest Hills and other garden spots of Queens could be reached by rapid transit after World War I, many members of the "better set" preferred to make a longer trip to the North Shore of Long Island or to Fairfield County on the Connecticut side of Long Island Sound. In a similar fashion, of course, the old Jersey suburban communities of Elizabeth, Rahway, and Roselle were eventually to fall into disfavor, as were those of the Bronx.

A suburban "style" had emerged on the American scene, and in many ways it was more than faintly repellent. The anti-urban bias, meaning anti-anything-or-anyone that did not fit the cut of the executive Protestant establishment and its followers among the middle class, expressed itself in various exclusionary practices which would bedevil American society for generations. The snobbishness, the air of contempt for the less fortunate, the openly racist real-estate policies and practices —these began to poison the air of the cities and their suburbs in the late 19th century. Gustav Kobbé, the Jersey Central publicist, expressed the general attitude as well as anyone:

> It may be said that thousands of the best citizens of New York are not citizens of that city at all. In the morning they flood the business districts of the metropolis; in the evening they ebb away. They are citizens of New York in so far as the city owes to their brains and energy a great share of its prosperity; they are not citizens in that they live and vote elsewhere. If this great suburban army of intelligent men lived as well as worked in New York, we would probably hear less of the necessity of municipal reform, for there would be just so much more intelligence among the voting population—which brings us back to our starting point: that of New York's best citizens thousands are, unfortunately for it, citizens of New Jersey, Long Island, and other suburban districts.

The suburban "tone" of the period was expressed in every phase of life—in clothing, architecture, social or recreational pastimes, and in transportation. This— the 1890s through the 1920s—was the time when private subscription passenger cars became *de rigueur*—from Greenwich, Connecticut; Pawling and Oyster Bay, New York; Morristown, Gladstone, Plainfield, and Red Bank, New Jersey; and elsewhere. The smart set, moving farther out into the country, even attempted to dictate a quaint design for their local stations. The timbered Tudor style was expressed in both commercial complexes and depots. It marked these public places as fit for the man in the Harris-tweed Brook Brothers suit and his Peck & Peck lady. Almost everywhere—on the North Shore of Chicago in Lake Forest and Winnetka; out in Philadelphia's Main-Line towns of Radnor and Wayne, or just as markedly in the estate areas of Abington and Cheltenham townships—the tone was English of

Club car, 1925.

the aristocratic sort. Wealthy Americans of British descent (and even some not so Waspish) had always imitated these upper-class manners and mores, but in the early years of the 20th century, Anglomania was lavishly expressed in Cotswold cottages and manorial estates, a passion for tweeds and brogues, riding to hounds, playing the golf course—in other words, in indulging a genteel country life untainted by urban concerns. Some say that the income tax brought an end to such indulgences, but it was more likely the Depression that sobered up the Prohibition generation. It was certainly the Depression that opened up parts of suburbia to such former aliens as successful Jewish businessmen, whose capital may have been reduced by the economic crisis but who now had an opportunity to buy some part of the lands which the Protestants were forced to subdivide.

The Depression also brought an end to the extension of suburban railroading. From 1930 on there was to be only a reduction in passenger traffic, a decline checked but temporarily by World War II and a gasoline shortage. Service was cut back drastically in many suburban areas. Until after the war, most people stayed put in the old bastions of affluence. A study of several thousand addresses listed in New York's 1934 *Social Register* may come as a surprise to today's social arbiter. A very high percentage of the elite still lived in such towns as Madison, Morristown, Short Hills, The Oranges, Elizabeth, Plainfield, and Englewood, New Jersey; Greenwich, Connecticut; Bronxville, Yonkers, Rye, Scarsdale, Hewlett, Flushing, and Great Neck, New York. Communities such as Bedford in upper Westchester county, Fairfield and Westport in Connecticut, and Far Hills and Bedminster in New Jersey—now so highly touted—hardly rated a notice. Not until after World War II did the tempo of suburbanization pick up again. By this time, of course, the automobile reigned supreme and the commuter lines were already close to bankruptcy or had already succumbed. Whole new towns developed along expressways, leaving those railroads which survived with only the remnants of their old clientele. No doubt the economic and political clout of wealthy suburban old-timers helped to salvage what was left of the railroads with public funds, but it was probably the further suburbanization of railroad exurbia, the "drawing in" to metropolitan areas of eastern Fairfield County, Connecticut; central Bucks County, Pennsylvania; and similar outposts of rusticity which at least gave the railroad executives a reason for running their trains beyond the fringes of the city.

The situation in the 1970s is healthier than it has been for years, but there are still extremely important decisions to be made about the direction of suburban development and the stabilization of the old commuter towns. For generations the commuter has been subsidized in his travel by the railroad. When there was still lots of land to be developed, and the railroad had an interest in it, the bargain struck with the passengers was beneficial for both parties. Now government agencies—acting for the public—are making up the losses. How much longer this will continue is questionable, but it is clear that rail travel is a great deal less expensive than the reconstruction or building and maintaining of highways. Private commuting by automobile, of course, may soon become a luxury. Use of the suburban rail lines has increased every year since the mid-1960s and, as in the case of the modern North Western in the 1960s, this service could even approach profitability if the lines are properly capitalized and managed. To what extent the public should underwrite the cost of living in suburbia, however, rather than devote more funds to the rebuilding of inner-city neighborhoods, is being energetically debated. The federal Department of Transportation, for instance, would like Amtrak to cease discounting weekly and monthly tickets on the so-called New York-Philadelphia "clockers," hourly trains running between the two cities with such limited stops as Princeton Junction, New Brunswick, Metro Park, and Newark in New Jersey. For many years, residents of Philadelphia's suburbs have commuted to New York on these expresses first established by the Pennsylvania.

The suburban system of the future will have to be more efficient in the use of energy, labor, and time. Many operational efficiencies have already resulted from the pooling of various private resources. Competing terminal facilities have been consolidated in some areas, and sections of trackage under the umbrella of Conrail or Amtrak are being shared in the New York-New Jersey area by former rivals, just as they were in the early years of the railroads when the building of viaducts or tunnels was too expensive for one company to bear. A few abandoned commuter lines may come back into operation, the West Shore which served the Hudson River communities of New Jersey and New York being a conspicuous and worthy example. A link between the Reading and Pennsylvania suburban terminals in Center-City Philadelphia is now being constructed, and this will result in more efficient use of expensive equipment.

It is unlikely that there will be further abandonment of service, yet service is sure to become more expensive. High-speed lines such as the Lindenwold which serves Camden, Haddonfield, and Lindenwold from Philadelphia via inner-city subway stations are one future form of commuter transport. Similar in concept is San Francisco's giant BART system. Still on the drawing board is a high-speed line to run from Newark to Plainfield, New Jersey. At stake in this extension of the PATH is the future of the Jersey Central commuter line it would parallel as far as Plainfield, and service to towns beyond this point. In 1959 Boston's Metropolitan Transit Authority began to operate rapid transit trains over the nine-mile Newton Highlands branch of the Boston & Albany, and this has since been made part of the enlarged Massachusetts Bay Transportation Authority system which also includes service on the other surviving suburban lines.

Not all suburban service of the future is likely to be directed to the city. As in the brief but glorious days of the interurbans during the early years of this century, the aim may be to provide rapid transit between shopping centers, industrial parks, and residential centers in outlying areas. Buses are now performing this service, and undoubtedly will continue to do so for some time to come. But the electric interurban may yet win the contest for efficient transport which it lost to the internal-combustion engine.

Whatever the future, suburban railroading as it has been known has little or no further route to travel. The average American downtown, however transformed by city planners, is being supplanted by the mall or shopping center. And despite the exhortations of ministers and politicians, corporations are inexorably moving their headquarters away from the old cities to the countryside or to new urban centers where the railroad has hardly ever carried anything more than freight. The commuter trains will continue, but their character will have changed. The names of the historic lines are already being submerged by a wealth of acronyms. The familiar colors—Penn red, New Haven blue, North Western yellow and green—are being painted over, and the symbols—Jersey Central's incomparable Statue of Liberty, the familiar Reading diamond, and Pennsylvania's keystone—gradually disappear under the streamlined initials of state, regional, and federal transportation agencies.

IV. Making the Best of It

Rarely has the average suburban commuter been termed what in truth he has been over the years—an inveterate malcontent. Even the most cynical and rude conductor or ticket agent has been reluctant to so damn his customers. No small number of retired railroad employees, in fact, speak of their often crazed passenger friends in a tone of fondness. Perhaps this is because almost from the beginning of time they have suffered together, because there has been a realization that "we're all in this together, fellows," and that one might as well make the best of it. A sort of gallows humor makes the trip bearable on the worst of days. Criticism, of course, is directed toward a common enemy of commuter and employee—"management." To sit on a train with a broken air-conditioning system below Pennsylvania Station on a sweltering hot day, on a train delayed so that the railroad president's private car can be attached—as was this writer's experience in the 1960s—is to have experienced the full measure of indignation. An official letter of complaint certainly would have been justified. Other complaints, however, are less reasonable—fares are never quite low enough, and rarely is service as rapid as desired. Now that most train service is being administered by public agencies, governmental officials and their bureaucrats are having to cope with both the unreasoning demands and legitimate complaints previously addressed to private management. The new public servants might relax a bit if they knew that this was all part of the commuting game. If the participants did not have a chance to gripe about playing according to someone else's rules, they wouldn't feel as if they were true suburbanites.

Traveling in a public pack has rarely been an especially ego-satisfying trip for the upwardly-mobile rail commuter. There are, of course, those private groups which pride themselves on special cars and services, but these social cliques have always been small in number, and there has been little opportunity to challenge the one-class structure of short-distance travel. No wonder, then, that many commuters have shown so much interest in the accoutrements of their daily trip—the cars and their appointments (or lack thereof), the stations and grounds, the personnel, and even the vehicles used to go to and from the depot. There is not the razzle-dazzle of big-time railroading, the glamor of streamliners which so excites rail fans. Rather, the interest is in the commonplace touches which help to make workaday life pleasant and engaging. The nature of the service is a trivial matter when compared with the meat-and-potatoes needs of the working man, but it is just such bourgeois concerns which lie very much at the heart of the suburban homing instinct that has drawn commuters away from the uncivilized city.

In the beginning it wasn't all that easy to make the trip in any sort of style. It was, however, an *exciting* experience. Fire power to carry passengers to and from suburban residences was supplied by wood, vast quantities of timber being readily available in the early 1800s. Train travel at that time was an extremely messy affair for any sort of passenger. Soot was an ever-present companion, and burning ashes could easily set both traveler and train afire. Charles Dickens described the situation well in *American Notes* (1842):

> On, on, on—tears the mad dragon of an engine with its train of cars; scattering in all directions a shower of burning sparks from its wood fire; screeching, hissing, yelling, panting, until at last the thirsty monster stops beneath a covered way to drink, the people cluster round, and you have time to breathe again.

Many city dwellers and country folk felt that the price of progress was too high. Typical of the railroad company accident reports is that from the Boston & Albany in 1869. Only deaths were given much space, and there were twenty-two that year. There wasn't room to list all of the accidents to person and property. On July 15, 1868, "Dennis Shehan, while walking upon the track at Wellesley, was struck by

Explosion of a locomotive, New York, New Haven & Hartford Railroad, 1891.

engine and killed"; later in the year, "William O'Neil fell between two platform cars in Boston, was run over and killed."

The streets of the cities and towns were filled with smoke from the engines, and in the country fences and woods were sometimes ravaged for fuel when supplies were low. Only gradually, in the mid-century, did coal come into use. And even then, trains left their marks on both riders and residents. The burning of anthracite helped considerably to lessen the pollution, but bituminous coal was cheaper to use and easier to obtain by the end of the century. Gradually cities banned the running of trains through certain sections. By the turn of the century the public had succeeded in forcing many companies to divert tracks through tunnels or over viaducts away from the flow of pedestrian and other traffic. As electrification was pursued in the early 1900s, further progress was made in cleaning up the railroad's acts. Finally, diesel power arrived to smooth out the ride on those lines which had not been electrified. All these changes were beneficial to the commuter. In many cases it meant a much faster trip. During and after the Depression, however, many railroads were forced to "go slow" in modernizing their fleets, and further electrification was postponed indefinitely. Until the 1950s, for instance, Chicago & North Western commuters jerked along behind chugging steam engines from another era. They weren't alone.

Passenger-car comfort and appointments have always been limited. In the 1870s and '80s, according to John White in *The American Railroad Passenger Car,* "For suburban, emigrant, or branch-line service, light, cheap cars were considered acceptable." Considering the slight or nonexistent profit to be made from this service, it is understandable why officials long relegated their dogs to the commuters. After the Civil War the parlor car was introduced for the comfort of the intercity passenger, and cars thus intended became fancier and fancier affairs. The commuter, however, continued to ride in quite undistinguished fashion. Seats were closely

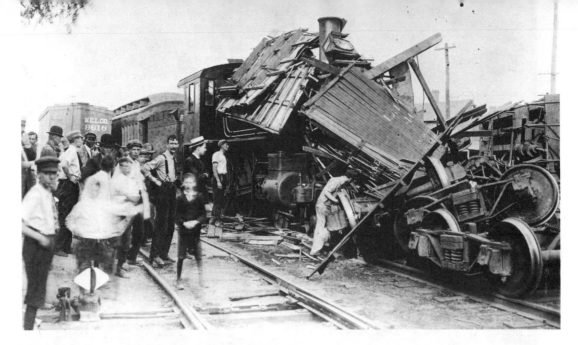

Wreck on the Long Island Railroad, Bay Shore, 1909.

"A Breakdown on the Road" by A.B Frost, 1889.

spaced and decoration was minimal. So, too, was heat and ventilation. Until the early 1900s, all passenger cars were made of wood or of wood reinforced with iron. There are commuters alive today who, with typical exaggerated pique, swear that they have ridden on such cars within the past twenty-five years.

If heat was available at all during a good part of the 19th century, it came from a wood- and, later, coal-burning stove which, in winter, might be placed in the middle of the car. Slowly, after 1890, a steam system linked to the locomotive pumped forth a modicum of warmth. Lighting on the early trains was first provided by candles, and, later in the century, by oil lamps and then gas. Reading a morning newspaper was certainly possible, but during much of the year the evening rush hour was a gloomy affair. Ventilation was always a problem on cars packed with passengers. The introduction of clerestory-roof cars in the 1870s helped to open up the space to more light and air, but a handful of smokers could defeat any system, even opened windows, if, indeed, they could be pried loose. Just when smokers were banned to their own fumes is uncertain, but segregation was probably an early practice.

Seats were never very comfortable affairs, but at least they were not of the wooden variety provided by second- or third-class European trains of the period. The reversible or "walkover" seat back was a standard feature in American cars very early. No one had to ride "backwards" in those days. To switch the backs was fun for the child taken to the city, and an automatic reflex of the conductor upon reaching the end of the run. Most seats were covered in mohair which, according to John White, was machine-made after 1882. Dusty remnants of this durable fabric can still be found on commuter cars. Other seats were covered with a woven rattan, a material almost as durable as mohair, but slippery rather than plush.

Early in the 1900s a revolution in passenger-car design occurred—the steel car was introduced. A safer container, it was less susceptible to fire and was thought at the time to be also less resistant to structural damage in accidents. Within a short period of time, several accordion-pleated specimens gave lie to the claim. All in all, however, the all-steel or rebuilt wooden car with steel framing was a decided improvement. The Long Island Railroad ordered 134 all-steel suburban cars from the American Car and Foundry Co. in 1904. The Long Island's managing company,

Passenger coach with wood stove, 1870s.

The smoking car, 1884.

the Pennsylvania, followed suit in 1907, the North Western in 1910, the Milwaukee Road a year later, and both the New Haven and New York Central substantially modernized their fleets in 1912. The Boston & Maine was one of the last to order the new equipment—in 1916—and as late as 1950 was still running 276 reinforced wooden cars.

During the 1920s a number of commuter lines purchased quite light passenger cars with arched rather than clerestory roofs. These were to be found on the Rock Island, Illinois Central, Boston & Albany, and the North Western. There was also experimentation with aluminum or a composite of that material and steel. In time, however, corrosion was discovered to be a particularly severe problem in those sections where aluminum members were joined to those of steel. Perhaps this is why the North Western trains of the 1940s—equipped with cars of this sort—were losing so many of their parts along the line. In the 1920s, however, things looked quite bright. The commuter's lot was about as good as it ever had been or would be again. Although cars were not air-conditioned, they were fitted with a low-pressure steam heating system, and with electric light. During the 1930s the railroads battled to keep their long-distance customers and experimented with stainless steel cars of a streamlined sort, but these advances hardly touched the commuter fleet. As John White explains, "The lightweights appeared . . . at a time when railroads could least afford a major investment in new equipment. The existing car fleet was adequate for

Interior of Baltimore & Ohio passenger coach with gas lamps, 1890.

the remaining traffic." And so it was to be for at least another fifteen to twenty-five years.

The electrification of such lines as the Illinois Central, Reading, Pennsylvania, Long Island, New Haven, Lackawanna, and New York Central during the first two decades of this century brought with it increased use of self-propelled cars. The MU or multiple-unit coaches built by Bethlehem Steel for the Reading have proved very durable over the years, as have the Pullman cars of the Illinois Central and the Lackawanna. The rail-diesel cars (RDC) of the post-World War II period used by some railroads have not begun to provide the space required for comfortable travel and have fallen into disfavor for this reason and because of technical problems. Better designed for the commuter routes are the bi-levels, first used in the late '40s on the Long Island and then rapidly adopted by the Chicago commuter lines. Seating as many as 169 passengers, they combine economy of operation with relative passenger ease.

Lighting of cars has been improved with the installation of indirect fluorescent fixtures on a number of lines. The bare-bulb look still prevails, however, in many areas of the Northeast where the old MU electric cars or steel products of the 1920s and '30s still hold sway. The situation is similar in regard to air conditioning. On new equipment, systems work fairly well; on the old cars, air conditioning is nonexistent or ebbs and flows with apparent disregard of the temperature. This has been a particularly difficult problem for the railroads to solve. "The passenger car," John White explains, "was as difficult to cool as it was to heat because of the large window area, frequently opened doors, short air throws, restricted power supply, and limited space for ducts and machinery."

The modernization of the railroad's motive power and passenger cars in recent years has been accompanied by a program of station improvement. The "solution" most often chosen, however, has been that of demolition. Inadequate "shelters" have been built on the ruins of proud depots in many areas. In other spots,

Pleasantville (New York) Station, New York Central, Harlem Division, c. 1900.

"remodeling" with cheap materials has ruined for all time what was once a structurally sound and architecturally-interesting building. Americans—often horrified by signs of old age—are only beginning to discover the cultural value of institutional structures which have served neighborhoods for many years and which can be "recycled." Many of the early stations were built for multiple purposes—as a post office and general store—and can be so utilized again. Almost all of the depots, as Victorian Americans preferred to call their local railroad buildings, provided an outpost for Western Union, and, when Railway Express was a going concern, it was a handy place for shipping packages or a trunk to summer camp or college. While there is no reason to go "down to the depot" today for such purposes, there are community needs which often can be met in this place—if it still exists.

Nearly every American community has waged a battle with its railroad company or companies regarding the upkeep of the station. In some cases, local improvement societies and garden clubs took upon themselves the job of beautifying the grounds. In others, private individuals underwrote the cost of providing a suitably tasteful station. For some of the early country gentlemen, it was a matter of pride and a sign of their social standing to have a proper gateway to their village. As Clay Lancaster has written, "The train station was the image of the community, presenting at a glance something about its size, affluence, livelihood, and social range of the citizens, their taste in architecture." The styles over the years have ranged from vernacular treatments of the Greek Revival through the Victorian Gothic and on to Renaissance Revival and the Beaux Arts. The stations of suburbia were nearly always more carefully designed and built than the average country or small-town depot.

In most respects, the terminal at the city end of the line was but a larger station, one that encompassed the needs of both suburban and long-distance travelers. Some railroads provided separate buildings or annexes for the use of suburban passengers. The majority of lines simply mixed service in the same structure, and assigned a block of tracks on a regular basis to the commuter runs. In either case, the terminal was as much home to the suburban commuter as it was to the intercity traveler. In its heyday, the terminal offered good food, attractive waiting areas for reading or writing, and perhaps even a movie or a game of bowling. Like the suburban station, it has been threatened with its very life. Fewer of these giant terminals, however, have been reduced to dust. Pennsylvania Station, of course, was unconscionably destroyed, but it is a tough job to demolish monuments of stone and mortar, and—for the time being—such enormous white elephants as South Station in Boston and the Reading Terminal in Philadelphia sit awaiting their fate.

"Baggage wagon adapted to country house use," Palmer-Moore Co., 1914.

It is impossible to leave this look at the physical elements of the commuter's world without mentioning at least briefly the one living artifact which has linked it to other spheres of transportation—the station wagon. Some of the earliest commuters practically lived along the tracks and close to the station. It made sense, despite the rush-hour noise and commotion. In any case, unless the town was on the main line, trains were not likely to disturb the country air for long. Later in the 19th century, not everyone could or wanted to be so conveniently situated. A horse and carriage was needed to deliver and pick up the daily traveler as well as visitors. Many Victorian stations were built with a graceful drive and *porte cochère* to accommodate the vehicle. Wagons were also used around the station—for hauling freight, baggage, and the mail. In the 20th century they were motorized. And soon they were available for the use of passengers.

A baggage wagon was the prototype. As *Town & Country* explained to its affluent readers in 1914, "While the ordinary passenger automobile has been developed to an extent that admits of few important improvements, the baggage wagon for all-round country use is still waiting to come into its own." Henry Ford was not the earliest to fill this need, but he was one of the most successful in the 1920s. Other car manufacturers quickly followed suit with wood and steel-bodied vehicles. The "woodie" was a familiar status symbol at the station by the 1940s. "For meeting guests at the station," Chevrolet enthused at the time, "it offers the perfect combination of smartness and utility." Ford's successful line of Country Squire wagons of the late '40s and early '50s provided many commuter families with just the right vehicle for shopping, taking the kids to school, and meeting the train. The old wood-sided models have since gone the way of wooden railroad passenger cars, safety and cost having dictated their replacement with metal.

Chevrolet station wagon, 1940.

New York

Grand Central Depot, New York City, c. 1880.

Reaching Out in Every Direction

Only during the 1830s and early '40s could anyone make sense of local railroad service in the New York area—there was so little of it. In 1836, for instance, nearly all the passengers in the tri-state region were being transported in one direction by one railroad company, the New York & Harlem—north to Yorkville and other early Manhattan outposts of country life. There was activity out in the boondocks, but it lacked scope. Less than ten years later, however, a vast cobweb of intersecting lines was being woven in and around the city. By 1850 the tracks of at least eight other railroads could be used to reach at least the outskirts of New York. At this time, men called "commuters" were traveling on "accommodation" trains that had been scheduled for the convenience of businessmen. In the decades following the Civil

War, suburban service became organized in a more formal manner, the terminus of nearly each line reaching farther and farther out into the country. Commuting by rail was an affordable expense for many businessmen and certainly for all passengers the fastest way to travel. And during much of the second half of the 19th century, a home in the country was a less expensive undertaking—despite the extra cost of transportation—than a residence in the city. Some commuters, of course, could and did afford both.

The lines of what would become in time the Erie, the Lackawanna, the Long Island, the New Haven, the Pennsylvania, and the Jersey Central systems in the New York area were laid in the 1830s through the '50s. Technology, financing, and political maneuvering determined their final form. Each line grew through merger

Grand Central Depot, train despatcher's office, New York City, 1875.

and careful development of regional freight and passenger traffic from the '50s until the 1890s. The Harlem and a line along the Hudson, the Hudson River Railroad, came under the control of Cornelius Vanderbilt in 1864. By 1868 this greatest railroad manager of all time had gained control of the New York Central, which then ran westward from Albany. There would be two further additions in the New York area during succeeding years. In 1885 a line which had bankrupted itself in a battle with the Vanderbilt system—the New York, West Shore & Buffalo Railway—ceded its route up the western side of the Hudson to the New York Central. Finally there was the acquisition in 1894 of the New York & Northern (the line that eventually became known as the Putnam Division), running between the Harlem and Hudson lines from Yonkers to Brewster.

In New Jersey the Pennsylvania Railroad and the Erie absorbed as much of the competition as possible, leaving only the Jersey Central and the Lackawanna as major independent companies. East of New York the Long Island Railroad kept growing larger and larger through the second half of the 19th century by acquiring a multitude of small lines, and at the turn of the century was itself swallowed up by the Pennsylvania. The Connecticut suburban territory has been synonymous with the New Haven system for many years, but during its formative years in the 1800s it was necessary for this large railroad company to buy out its competition any number of times.

These major rail carriers bridged, tunneled, and ferried their way across the highly varied regional landscape. Without question their number-one priority was that of capturing and serving as much of the industrial and agricultural New York-area market as was possible. At the same time, however, the railroads listened to the pleas of small towns and villages for passenger as well as freight service. And all the companies showed a keen interest in residential real estate. Some took a direct hand in building up villages as suitable suburban colonies. In the case of almost every rail line, moreover, there were already existing towns—market centers—that were important to reach and to connect with the city. To determine today just why one route to or from such a town was chosen over another would take a careful reading of the minutes of thousands of board meetings. Geography certainly had something to do with such decisions. The railroads first took a path of least resistance, and then gradually tackled the job of removing as many of the natural barriers as was humanly and financially possible. Not until tunnels were opened under the Hudson and East rivers in the early 1900s did the effort to move mountains begin to ebb. Then increasing attention was given to the means of conveyance—steam propulsion versus electrification—rather than to the path to be followed.

New York's railroad suburbia, then, emerged and was to sustain itself for many years for a number of economic and geographic reasons. Politics, too, had its place. Railroads were chartered to serve a set area, and changes in the approved plan of operation—mergers, rates, routes—often occasioned time-consuming and bitter battles that could be won only by playing the game of politics. Yet there is one more element in the development of New York suburban railroading which has to be considered—the social. The majority of the men who ran the lines became commuters. They like their brothers—the money managers, the merchandisers,

Shelter and overhead footbridge, Bedford Park, The Bronx, New York City, New York Central & Hudson River Railroad, 1893.

and the lawyers—wanted to live the "good life" that suburbia promised. And they made sure that the trains would be there to serve them and their neighbors.

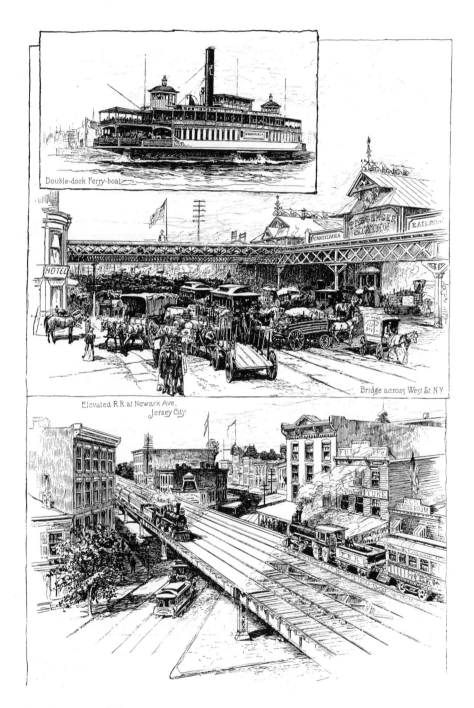

Pennsylvania Railroad, 1890. From top: *double-deck ferry boat crossing the Hudson River; bridge across West Street, New York City; elevated railroad at Newark Ave., Jersey City, New Jersey.*

The New York Central Railroad

Harlem Division

The early commuters on the New York & Harlem paid little for their transport, the cost to Harlem or Mott Haven being only about 4¢ each way. Today's traveler bound for Westchester County who rides below much of Park Avenue and above and below a large portion of the Bronx pays out a much higher proportion of his income for the daily trip—with good reason. The good old days were not the 1840s, as New York Central historian Alvin Harlow explains in his history of the railroad:

> At 26th Street, about 15 minutes before the leaving time of a train, the starter seized an iron bolt about a foot long with a nut on the end, and banged violently on an iron plate set in the top panel of the door leading from the waiting room to the platform. . . . He then opened the door, allowing passengers access to the train. . . ."

HARLEM RAILROAD.—Williams' Bridge and White Plains Trains.

Miles	Fares	NEW YORK to WHITE PLAINS. TRAINS LEAVE.	1st Tr'n	2d Tr'n	3d Tr'n	4th Tr'n	5th Tr'n	6th Tr'n	7th Tr'n	8th Tr'n	9th Tr'n	10th Tr'n	11th Tr'n	12th Tr'n	13th Tr'n	14th Tr'n	15th Tr'n
			AM.	AM.	AM.	AM.	AM.	AM.	P.M.	P.M.	P.M.	P.M.	P.M.	P.M.	P.M.	P.M.	P.M.
		....City Hall.....	7 00	8 15	8 40	9 30	11 40	2 15	3 00	3 30	4 00	4 20	5 00	5 45	6 15	8 00	11 00
3	6	.....32d Street.....	7 30	8 45		10 00			3 30		4 30	4 50	5 30	6 15	6 45	8 30	11 30
6	12	.....Yorkville.....	7 40		9 20	10 10	12 22	2 55		4 09		5 00	5 39	6 25	6 54	8 40	11 40
8	15	.....Harlem......	7 50		9 30	10 20	12 31	3 05		4 18		5 10	5 48	6 35	7 04	8 50	11 50
9	15	....Mott Haven...	7 54		9 34	10 24	12 37	3 09		4 22		5 14	5 51	6 39	7 08	8 54	11 54
10	18	...Morrisania ...	8 02		9 42	10 32	12 48	3 17		4 30		5 22	5 58	6 47	7 18	9 02	12 02
12	23	.....Fordham	8 10		9 50	10 40	1 00	3 25		4 37	5 01	5 30	6 05	6 55	7 25	9 10	12 10
14	30	.Williams' Bridge	8 15	9 15	9 55	10 45	1 10	3 30		4 45	5 05	5 35	6 15	7 00	7 30	9 15	12 15
17		...Hunt's Bridge...	---	9 21	---	---	1 20	---		4 52	5 15	---	6 22	---	7 37		
19	49	.....Tuckahoe.....		9 30			1 34			5 02	5 26		6 32		7 47		
22	56	.....Scarsdale.....		9 35			1 45			5 10	5 33		6 38		7 53		
24		Hart's Corners..		9 38			1 52			5 14	5 38		6 42		8 57		
26	65	White Plains.Arr.		9 45			2 00		4 00	5 20	5 45		6 50		8 00		

Miles	Fares	WHITE PLAINS To NEW YORK. TRAINS LEAVE.	1st Tr'n	2d Tr'n	3d Tr'n	4th Tr'n	5th Tr'n	6th Tr'n	7th Tr'n	8th Tr'n	9th Tr'n	10th Tr'n	11th Tr'n	12th Tr'n	13th Tr'n	14th Tr'n	15th Tr'n
			AM.	AM.	AM.	AM.	AM.	AM.	P.M.	P.M.	P.M.	P.M.	P.M.	P.M.	P.M.	P.M.	P.M.
		...White Plains...	5 00		7 00		9 05		12 40		2 30			6 10		8 00	
2		..Hart's Corners..	5 03		7 07		9 10		12 45		2 38			6 16			
4		.....Scarsdale.....	5 08		7 12		9 15		12 45		2 46			6 21			
7		.....Tuckahoe.....	5 16		7 25		9 30		12 55		2 59			6 32			
9		..Hunt's Bridge...	5 23		7 28		9 38		1 04		3 18			6 40			
12		.Williams' Bridge.	5 30	6 40	7 35	8 30	9 45	10 10	1 10	1 15	3 30	5 05	6 09	6 50	7 15	8 25	9 00
14		.....Fordham.....	5 35	6 45	7 40	8 35	9 50	10 15		1 20	3 40	5 10	6 05	6 55	7 20		9 05
16		....Morrisania ...	5 43	6 53	7 47	8 43		10 23		1 29	3 52	5 18	6 13	7 03	7 28		9 12
17		....Mott Haven...	5 51	7 01	7 54	8 51		10 31		1 36	4 02	5 26	6 21	7 11	7 36		9 21
18		.....Harlem......	5 55	7 05	8 02	8 55		10 35		1 40	4 08	5 30	6 25	7 15	7 40		9 25
20		.....Yorkville.....	6 05	7 15	8 10	9 05		10 45		1 50	4 18	5 40	6 35	7 25	7 50		9 35
23		... 32d Street.....															10 35
26	65	... City Hall..Arr.	6 45	7 55	8 50	9 45	10 45		2 10	2 30		6 20	7 15	8 05	8 30	9 25	10 15

Timetable, New York & Harlem Railroad, 1855.

The next step in the starting-up ritual on the Harlem and other early railroads was the ringing of the station bell hung in the roof five minutes before departure time, and this signal often attracted a crowd of neighborhood fans. Perhaps these were the first "train-watchers" who would haunt depots and terminals for years to come. The ringing, according to Harlow, "was repeated at one-minute intervals until leaving time, when at the last stroke, the engine was supposed to start."

From time to time, of course, the engine had not developed enough steam with which to jerk forward, and the whole procedure had to be repeated. Once underway, the trip might pass uneventfully. The accommodations, however, were primitive at best. The cars were of wood, and lighted by candle. Heat—in the form of cast-iron stoves—was a sometime thing in the winter. In the summertime the closest approximation to air conditioning was provided by a water boy. As Harlow explains:

> The water-boy . . . dispensed his cool drinks by pouring the ice water from a gooseneck kettle into a circle of tumblers set in a castor or cruet-frame such as were used to adorn dinner tables. It was considered the decent thing, after you drank, to drop a penny in the castor.

By the 1850s and '60s, commuters to Westchester and beyond were riding in considerably more comfort. Fordham, in what is now the north Bronx, was reached in 1841, White Plains in late 1844, Croton Falls by 1847, and the link-up with the Western Massachusetts Railroad (later the Boston & Albany) at Chatham in 1852.

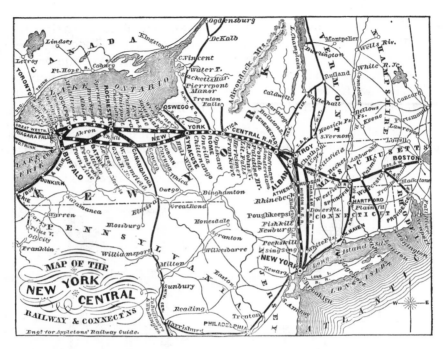

New York Central Railway, 1866.

In 1840 the New York State legislature had given permission to the Harlem to extend its tracks as far north as Chatham and to establish a branch eastward from Williamsbridge in lower Westchester to connect with the New York & New Haven, precursor of the New York, New Haven & Hartford. In 1848 the first through train from New Haven to New York ran through Rye, Harrison, Mamaroneck, New Rochelle, Pelham, Mount Vernon, and then, in a southernly direction via the Harlem tracks, to the city.

Service to Mott Haven, Melrose, Morrisania, Tremont, Fordham, and Williamsbridge, was extremely important in the early years. Many families became established in this area of lower Westchester in the mid-1800s. An 1867 publication, *Walling's Route and City Guides, Harlem Route,* describes the village of Melrose (162nd Street) as then being "laid out in city lots and streets," and "rapidly growing." This was true of other nearby areas which in former times had been the rather exclusive province of wealthy landowners such as the Morris and Van Cortlandt families. The scenery along the Bronx River was especially beautiful and excited the interest of early real-estate promoters. The arcadia that could be reached via Mott Haven station (138th Street) in the 1860s was thus described:

> We pass through what is at present a charmingly rural region; green, grassy lawns, forest trees, rugged rocks, and the beautifully clear Bronx river, are combined in a series of many elegant and commodious villas and cottages, surrounded by walks, drives and gardens.

Beyond the limits of what is now the Bronx were other areas of rapid suburban development. Mount Vernon—after 1848 the first town to be reached beyond the Harlem-New Haven junction—was prime real-estate territory. It has been said that the town "owes its very existence to the railroad." Building lots were plotted in 1851 in an area south of the New Haven tracks by a group of New Yorkers organized as the New York Industrial Home Association No. 1. At the same time, the Teutonic Homestead Association of New York was establishing the village of West Mount Vernon along the Harlem tracks. By 1854 there were nearly 2,000 residents in the two sections, and a third area, Central Mount Vernon, was being built up. By 1878 all three villages were tied together to form what is now known as Mount Vernon. Although small manufacturing plants were established at an early date throughout this area, a large group of male residents journeyed to Manhattan each of the six working days. The train was the only way to go. Unfortunately, the railroad was not better equipped to handle the demand for service in the mid-1800s than it is today. As Alvin Harlow writes:

Harlem suburban trains were so long and so crowded that conductors couldn't work through fast enough, and slick commuters were buying dime tickets to

Bronx Park Station, New York Central, Harlem Division, 1900.

Park Avenue, New York City, view south of 56th Street where tracks were being depressed for electric service, 1905.

49

Harlem or Mott Haven, boarding the rear car and riding to their homes several stations farther than they had paid for. The railroad finally checkmated these fellows by putting another conductor on the rear cars and stopping the train to eject any passenger found riding beyond his ticket.

Neither commuters nor the railroads have changed that much.

In the 1870s a connection between the Hudson River Railroad and the Harlem was completed at Mott Haven, and passenger trains no longer (except a vestigial remnant) ran down the West Side of Manhattan but followed the Harlem route to Grand Central Terminal along with the New Haven trains. The first great 42nd Street station was finished in 1871; by 1876 the Park Avenue tunnel was completed and effectively buried from view a good portion of the multi-line trackage south of Harlem. Two years earlier the Morrisania, West Farms, and Kingsbridge sections of the Bronx—formally known as the "Annexed District"—had been added to the city. There were over 30,000 residents at the time, a goodly number of whom visited Grand Central each day. Not until 1895 would the remaining northern villages—some forty-five in number—be annexed.

In the 1890s and early 1900s considerable real-estate development was occurring in the still green country territory north of Woodlawn Cemetery. As the northern Bronx began to fill up slowly with small houses and flats, the person seeking room to build a stylish country home looked toward Bronxville, Scarsdale, and beyond White Plains to Pleasantville, Chappaqua, and Mt. Kisco. To some extent, this had been summer-home territory, convenient to New York in warm months for the New York businessman who wished to give his family all the benefits of fresh air. The far-northern stretches after White Plains continued to be popular spots for summer bungalows and cabins for many years later. In this respect, the Harlem line was not unique. Almost everywhere in the country, pleasure spots for the day or weekend excursion opened up by the railroad became, in time, residential suburban territory. Railroad executives encouraged settlement by *first* building seasonal facilities such as hotels and picnic grounds. Permanent residents were soon to follow.

Bronxville, despite its close proximity to the sprawling city, managed to maintain its air of country gentility for many years after the economic boom of the pre-World War I period. Development was carefully controlled, and what public disapproval could not prevent, formal zoning codes prohibited. A publication of the Harlem Division spoke with approval in 1890 of "Armour Hill Park," "on a pretty hillside to the left of the track, within three minutes' walk of the . . . station," which was "being rapidly improved by the erection of numerous tasteful dwellings." These homes were being built by prominent New Yorkers as year-round residences, although some families may have also maintained Manhattan town houses or apartments.

Beyond White Plains was countryside attractive enough to draw the interest of extremely wealthy gentlemen farmers whose business in the city did not require constant attention. Pawling and Bedford were centers of exurban activity early in the 1900s. Daily commutation was not a necessity. Trains stopping at these stations were not as frequent as those serving the area south of White Plains or even the villages of Pleasantville and Mt. Kisco which lie between White Plains and Bedford. This latter area, as described by a Harlem Division propagandist in the 1890s, was said to be a place where "Rare combinations of mountain, stream, and foliage greet the eye in endless variety, the whole forming a panorama of rural scenery incomparable for beauty, picturesqueness, and variety." Not surprisingly, the prose used to describe areas of the Bronx in the 1850s is almost identical.

Northern Westchester in the 1920s became *the* desirable territory for certain harried New York businessmen and their families. What had constituted a private sanctuary for the very rich and some natives, however, soon developed as an affordable alternative for the upper-middle-class family that had to be satisfied with only one residence. Mt. Kisco was especially favored. Even the mortality statistics of the time appeared to champion the hilly locale. They proved, in the words of a railroad spokesman, that Mt. Kisco was "more than twice as healthy as the great metropolis." Most suburban towns, however, were similarly well off at the time.

As these northern villages began to grow, those south of White Plains started to absorb more and more of the city's middle class. The electrification of the line from Grand Central to North White Plains in the early 1900s may not have created a greater demand for service, but it meant a smoother, less troublesome ride. Fires in the Park Avenue tunnels would still occur (as even a 1970s commuter will gladly testify), but the removal of the steam locomotive as early as 1906 from the environs of the new Grand Central (the third such building), hastened the arrival of rapid service which resembled more and more that offered by the streetcar and elevated companies. During peak hours there were trains to White Plains nearly every fifteen minutes.

After reaching a peak in ridership and service in 1929, the railroad began its long descent into the hell of bankruptcy. World War II offered some sort of reprieve since gasoline for automobiles was in such short supply. The postwar period can only be described as dismal, and the New York Central's merger with the Pennsylvania Railroad barely improved the situation. Now operated by New York State's Metropolitan Transportation Authority and Conrail, the division and its transport potential is being taken seriously once again, and ridership has been climbing.

The founders of the New York & Harlem intended their line to link the city with Albany and the West. By the late 1840s it was clear that the Hudson River Railroad could more effectively provide this connected service. Twenty years later, in the late '60s, Commodore Vanderbilt made sure that this route—connected with the Harlem at Mott Haven—was fully utilized as the main line. The Harlem remains of interest to railroad historians, however, not because of its links to other markets, but because it was the first working route out of New York and would provide the right of way for at least two other railroads. The Harlem, then, was the pioneer. It was also the first of the urban railroads to become almost completely suburbanized. Communities along its path developed more rapidly than those in eastern Long Island, on the Hudson in eastern Westchester, or across the river in New Jersey.

Hudson Division

During the 1840s residents of the old Hudson River villages of Dobbs Ferry and Tarrytown were not at all interested in having trains disturb the tranquil country air. Besides, there was excellent steamboat service to both New York and Albany. Perhaps more than any other outlying area of New York City, the towns of Westchester along the Hudson guarded their privacy. From the earliest time of Dutch settlement in the 17th century, large tracts of land had been kept intact as manorial preserves, and the style of the patroons was handed down to generations of valley residents and rubbed off on their retainers. Still, the railroad came—the

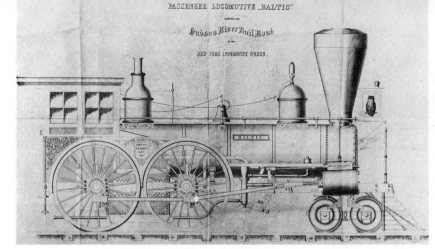

The "Baltic," locomotive built for the Hudson River Railroad by the New York Locomotive Works, 1854.

Hudson River Railroad—and in 1846 work was begun on the new route to Albany from the city. Poughkeepsie was reached in 1849, and East Albany, across the river from the capital, two years later. The New York City terminal was located at Chambers Street on the lower West Side.

Until 1871, when the Hudson tracks were rerouted to the Harlem via a connecting line in the Bronx between Spuyten Duyvil and Mott Haven, all the Hudson trains proceeded down the West Side of Manhattan or, as it was often called then, New York Island. What they passed through along this original route were not, except in the southern extreme, city streets, but sparsely settled lands. "Approaching New York," Alvin Harlow has written, "the track crossed the mouth of Spuyten Duyvil Creek and ran . . . past the pleasant suburbs of Inwood and Manhattanville, where there were some beautiful estates on or near the foot of those Highlands which make upper Manhattan noteworthy." The Bronx neighborhood of Riverdale—if stripped today of its post-World War II apartment towers—might suggest something of the pastoral situation of upper Manhattan's early settlements. Before and after the route change, Riverdale was served by the line, but upper Manhattan was left with only a few shuttle trains between Chambers Street and Spuyten Duyvil, service which continued because of state charter obligations until the early 1900s. This valuable Manhattan trackage, however, was and is still utilized for freight.

Commodore Vanderbilt assumed control of the Hudson and the Harlem lines in 1864. By November of 1869, the New York Central & Harlem River Railroad had emerged as a corporate entity. The main line of the nation's most important east-west carrier then passed through territory along the Hudson which was perfectly situated for suburban development of the sort that had already occurred in upper Manhattan and along the Harlem line in the eastern section of Manhattan and in the central Bronx. As anyone driving through much of the western portion of Westchester County today can see for himself, it is remarkable that the landscape has not been more drastically altered over the years. Even the tracks of the main line seem to have been hidden away in much of the hilly riverfront. Suburbia, however, was on its way as early as the 1850s. Then there was one "milk train" and eleven full-fledged locals that plied their way from Albany to New York and back. Contrary to general impressions, the milk train was not only a convenience for the dairyman, but also served the commuter who at the time had to be an "early bird" as well as a night owl. By 1869 there were eight special local trains in the morning to New York from Poughkeepsie, Peekskill, Sing Sing, Tarrytown, and Yonkers and five returning in the late afternoon or early evening. These locals supplemented the main-line express service which included stops at some of the suburban stations.

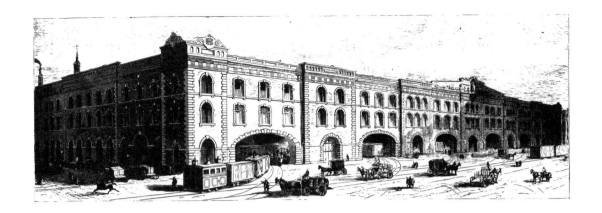

Hudson River Railroad Depot, Hudson Street, New York City, 1869.

Village of Manhattanville, New York, 1834, as sketched by J.W. Hill.

New York Central & Hudson River Railroad Station, 138th Street, New York City, 1885.

"Lyndhurst," Tarrytown, New York, 1965, the home of the Gould family.

Ardsley-on-Hudson (New York) Station, New York Central, Hudson division, c. 1910.

Commuting developed, however, more slowly on the Hudson line than on the Harlem. Thoughout the years it has never attained the volume achieved by the latter division. Growth along much of the Hudson was more measured and in keeping with the stately ways of the area. Even as late as 1893, such communities as Riverdale, Mount St. Vincent, and the Glenwood section of Yonkers were presented in a New York Central brochure as ideal country sites for suburban villas. Each community was uncomfortably close to the city's sprawl, but upper-middle-class residents were pictured living amidst estate dwellers in perfect harmony and contentment. It was as if the Phillipses and Beekmans and other members of the landholding aristocracy were still reading the Lesson on Sunday morning at the English Gothic church, and perhaps they were.

The privileged position of many of the Hudson River villages has been maintained until the present time. The same pressures of population growth and industrialization which have so changed much of the early suburban landscape elsewhere were nonetheless to be felt along the river—first in the immediate area of Yonkers, made a city in 1872, and then gradually farther and farther north. During the 1870s such settlements as Irvington, Dobbs Ferry, and Tarrytown became incorporated villages. They were fast becoming commuter towns. Many of the first families stayed in place, but others were moving on to the north and more open country. By the end of the century, the suburban territory included such distant communities as Garrison and Cold Spring. The "gilded age" was over for even the Goulds and Van Rensselaers, and a semblance of social democracy was emerging in lower Westchester as more and more large tracts of land were broken into smaller parcels for Colonial Revival and English Tudor homes on "manageable" acres. Some of these were second or country weekend residences, but many represented the only investment in real estate that the owner could afford to make. It would not be long before apartment houses would come to such villages as Irvington, for example, to be carefully nestled in landscaped hillsides convenient to the railroad station. During the Depression, simple economic necessity forced the abandonment of a good portion of the grandest estates, the land being sold to developers for pleasant, but modest by

Hudson House, Ardsley-on-Hudson, New York, 1937, with covered walk to station at right.

1930s standards, suburban homes. And so the trend has continued ever since. The subdivisions of the early 1900s are now being broken up once again for yet smaller plots. But because the area has developed with so little haste, major corporations have found it a tasteful and convenient retreat for their executive headquarters. In this case, suburbia has managed to make the city agree to its own terms. But, as with Greenwich, Connecticut, things are not quite the same in the corporate 1970s as they were before expressways brought the city even closer. Automobile traffic, for example, is strangling most of these once-small villages.

As with most major commuter lines in the past decade, there has been an increase in patronage after many years of decline. The peak of passenger traffic was reached in the late 1920s. By then the Hudson line had been electrified as far as Croton Harmon and considerably improved in equipment. Only those passengers traveling back and forth from such stations as Peekskill or Garrison were inconvenienced by the switching between steam and electric power. In 1930 there were seven morning and evening rush hour trains between Croton Harmon and Grand Central Terminal. Approximately the same number of trains also served the Glenwood and central stations of Yonkers, and others to the south—Mount St. Vincent, Riverdale, Spuyten Duyvill, Marble Hill, and High Bridge. Stops at 138th Street (Mott Haven) and 125th Street (Harlem) were usually made only to discharge passengers. Since the Hudson Division also served as the New York Central's main line, many commuters could also take advantage of this passenger service.

Putnam Division

The story of the Putnam Division of the New York Central is that of a railroad that no one really wanted for many years—except for the commuters who had settled in its path. Running northeasterly from Yonkers through Westchester and Putnam counties roughly midway between the Harlem and Hudson Divisions, it started life

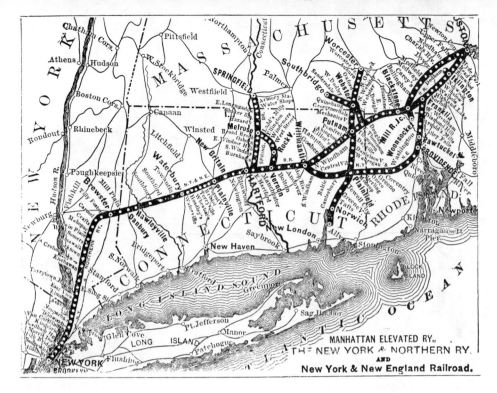

New York & Northern Railway, 1893.

in the 1870s as the New York & Northern Railway. It never produced a profit for its stockholders. When its merger with the New York Central came in 1894, a number of Yonkers businessmen were considerably richer than they had been in years. How they pulled off the sale is one of the more amusing chapters in the fading years of the railroad barons.

The New York & Northern made the New Haven Railroad nervous. The latter's monopoly of the New York to Boston market was being challenged in the '80s and early '90s by an upstart subsidiary of the Reading system—the New York & New England Railroad which ran from Fishkill-on-Hudson to Boston. For some time the New York & Northern advertised its link with the New York & New England at Brewster in Putnam County. What better way for freight and passengers to be hauled from New York City to Boston and intermediate central New England towns than via the New York & Northern tracks? At no time did many customers take advantage of the service even though rates were slashed to make it more attractive. The New Haven's shore route was less direct, but it was much better equipped and maintained. There really was no great threat, then, to the New Haven's virtual monopoly. But because the giant railroad company thought so, and because the New York Central was such a good and close friend, the New York & Northern was annexed and became known as the Putnam Division. The commuters along the line were only pawns in the game, but at least there was new money to throw into the operation. As it turned out—years later, however—the annexation was good money following bad. The New Haven put an end to the complete New York & New England system in 1895 by buying up the latter's bankrupt properties.

The route taken by the New York & Northern prior to its acquisition was an extremely circuitous one on the New York end. Over the lines of the Manhattan Elevated Railway (Ninth Avenue Elevated), a company controlled by the New York & Northern, one could travel to the Polo Grounds at 155th Street and there

Terminus of Manhattan Elevated Railway (Ninth Avenue Elevated) at Polo Grounds, 155th Street, New York City, 1890s.

change to a rapid transit train destined for Getty Square, Yonkers. Undoubtedly many commuting residents of the central northern Bronx (as yet to be annexed to the city) found this a convenient means of transport. Stops were made at High Bridge, Morris Dock, Fordham Heights, Kingsbridge, and Van Cortlandt; service during rush hour was scheduled for every half-hour. At Getty Square the passenger traveling further on transferred to a regular New York & Northern train. Several stops were made in outlying sections of Yonkers, at Ardsley (not Ardsley-on-Hudson which was served by the Hudson line), Elmsford, and the eastern section of Tarrytown (East View), with most trains ceasing their run at Pocantico Hills, twenty miles from 155th Street. A few trains served the Brewster terminus, and such summer vacation spots as Lake Mahopac and Carmel both before and after the 1894 merger.

The New York Central rerouted the New York & Northern trains from the Yonkers terminus to Grand Central and directed them on the Harlem tracks as far north as High Bridge. Here there was a link with Sedgwick Avenue and the Bronx Terminal Market stations. From High Bridge north the railroad was rerouted to skirt Getty Square (served, as before, by the Hudson Division), stopping at Lincoln, Dunwoodie Park, and on along the old trackage. Pocantico Hills was dropped from the schedule and Graham added; Yorktown Heights became the terminus of most trains rather than Pocantico Hills. Brewster, already reached by the Harlem Division, faded in importance as a Putnam division stop.

During the early 1900s the central Westchester area grew tremendously; extension of many trains from Pocantico Hills to Yorktown Heights was necessitated by an increase in ridership. But then came the automobile, the Saw Mill River Parkway, and the Depression. Never very strong to begin with, the Putnam Division subsided into near collapse. It is miraculous that the line survived as long as it did—until 1957. A petition to cease passenger service was filed with New York State in that year, and approval was given for a March 12, 1958, cut-off date. By October of '57, however, there were no trains running. During the 1950s everything could and did happen to commuters and their railroads. The New York Central's management, then headed by the incomparable Alfred Perlman, just decided to throw the switch a little early. When New York State and Conrail came to the rescue of the railroads in the 1970s, there was nothing much left of the New York & Northern.

Getty Square Station, Yonkers, New York, New York & Northern Railway, 1890.

Van Cortlandt Park Station, New York & Northern Railway, the Bronx, New York City, 1890s.

The West Shore Railroad

The West Shore is the only division of the New York Central which served suburbs in New Jersey and those in Rockland and eastern Orange counties of New York. The West Shore is no more, and it is questionable whether the Vanderbilt system was ever deeply concerned about the line's survival. It began in 1880 as an independent company, the New York, West Shore & Buffalo Railway, and as a bold challenge to the New York Central's link to the Midwest via Buffalo. At this time the giant system controlled the Lake Shore & Michigan Southern Railway between Buffalo and Chicago via Cleveland and Toledo. The New York Central did not need competition on its "Water Route" west, and did not welcome the possibility of a Midwestern railroad linking up with the West Shore at Buffalo. Although the battle between the little giant and the mammoth attracted the interest of the public, it was not much of a contest. The West Shore was poorly financed, and in 1885 the New York Central took over the bankrupt route for a term of 475 years.

Nearly 480 miles of trackage were acquired, and that which paralleled the New

York Central main line was slowly abandoned. As late as 1930 a few trains still ran on West Shore tracks from Rochester and Buffalo and over other upstate branches. Basically, however, what was retained was valuable suburban property as well as a link from New York to the Catskills via a branch line at Kingston. Among the properties purchased were the ferry boats which ran from West 42nd Street in Manhattan to a brand new terminal at Weehawken.

Most of the suburban trains run by the original company terminated their runs at West Haverstraw, New York, and the New York Central continued this policy. There were, however, several trains each day that continued on to the historic towns of Newburgh and Cornwall on the Hudson. The whole area from Stony Point to Highland, including Bear Mountain, was a popular one for weekend excursions by rail. The West Shore had spared no expense in tunneling through the mountains in the West Point/Haverstraw area. The core of the suburban service lay in New Jersey and in adjoining New York State towns—Little Ferry, Ridgefield Park, Teaneck, Orangeburgh, Blauvelt, West Nyack, Valley Cottage, Congers, and Haverstraw. As was the case on the other side of the Hudson in the 1890s and early decades of the 20th century, farmland slowly gave way to residential development, old Dutch barns to solid middle-class cottages.

West Shore Railway Terminal and tunnel, Weehawken, New Jersey, 1884.

The Depression did not badly affect the operation of the West Shore. In 1930 there were eight morning and seven evening rush hour trains serving the suburban territory; six years later schedules had actually improved. For suburbanites from Bergen and Rockland counties, the Weehawken terminal made good sense. The Jersey City and Hoboken crossings used by the other railroads were convenient only for travelers coming from the west and south. The Hudson & Manhattan Railroad tubes (now the PATH) were similarly out of the way.

West Shore Railway and Central Railroad of New Jersey ferry terminals, 42nd Street, New York City, 1939.

After World War II, the West Shore's health declined and finally—in the mid '50s—all service was abandoned. The primary reason seems clear—the automobile. Bergen County's first important highway link to New York was established in 1931 with the opening of the George Washington Bridge; the Lincoln Tunnel provided a second route in 1937 which almost paralleled the Weehawken 42nd Street crossing. In the 1950s the Tappan Zee Bridge and the New York State Thruway opened up Rockland County for extensive real-estate development. While the automobile may be blamed for the demise of the railroad, there is no evidence that the New York Central effectively utilized the suburban line or defended it against the encroachments of the internal-combustion engine. Thousands of new residents crossed the Hudson after World War II in search of homes and the vast majority of these new commuters elected to travel by car. No one, it seems, could forsee the day when approaches to the bridges and tunnels would back up with cars for miles each weekday morning and evening. Now, at last, there is talk that the West Shore may be revived. If state and federal government is going to subsidize mass transportation as it has the driver of the car, truck, or bus, then the revival of the rail commuter line may be the best investment.

WEST SHORE STATION
HIGHLAND, N.Y.

Highland (New York) Station, West Shore Railway, c. 1900.

The New York, New Haven & Hartford Railroad

Here stand dozens of diesel road and yard locomotives abandoned to the weather, rusting and in various stages of disintegration. Some are simply cannibalized locomotive carcasses. Others are intact but with the exhaust fan roof grilles open, admitting rain and snow to the machinery inside. In numerous instances, cab doors and engine shutters are wide open to wind-blown dirt as well as weather....

Commuters in the New Haven's New York and Connecticut territory will not be surprised to learn that the scene described so graphically is that of the Cedar Hill Yard outside New Haven. The year was 1960, a time when the railroad had reached the depths of its desperation, and had nowhere to go. The description is found in a landmark report issued by the Connecticut Public Utilities Commision. In the following year the railroad was declared bankrupt, and in 1962 the trustees filed a

61

petition to allow the line to be merged with the Penn-Central corporation. Agreement was reached on the purchase of the railroad's assets in 1965, and finally on January 1, 1969, the New Haven was formally absorbed by the short-lived New York-Philadelphia combine. Trains continued to run during the period of bankruptcy—some of them, at least, some of the time—just as they had in earlier eras of economic crisis. In the 1970s the states of New York and Connecticut, assisted by Conrail, realized that it was in their best interest not only to keep the trains running, but to improve their operation.

Throughout the 20th century the New Haven has been plagued with financial troubles and, most often, less than adequate executive talent with which to meet them. Lower-echelon employees, however, stayed loyal to the line and provided the mechanical first aid required for a patient slowly losing his functions. A remarkable number of commuters also remained steadfast, if not resigned, during the worst years of the post-World War II period. The railroad was so much a part of their lives that they could not schedule their daily lives without it. As Archie Robertson in *Slow Train to Yesterday* puts it, "The existence of the train itself was always taken for granted until it died." In the case of the New Haven, death could not be the final answer.

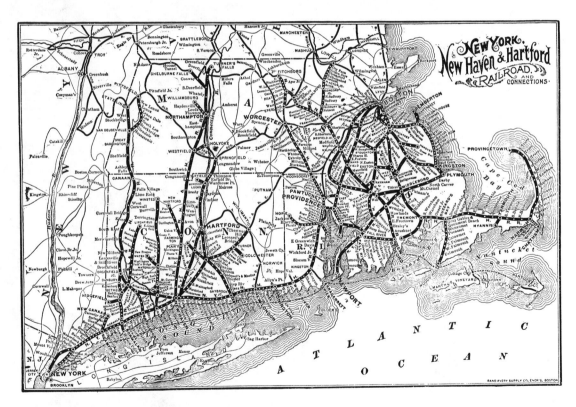

New York, New Haven & Hartford Railroad, 1893.

The development of the eastern part of Westchester County, New York, and the western section of Fairfield County, Connecticut, parallels in many respects the progress of the New Haven during the 19th and early 20th centuries—its main line

Rye (New York) Station, New York, New Haven & Hartford Railroad, 1885.

to the city. Since 1847 when the link with the New York & Harlem was completed at Williamsbridge in what is now the Bronx, it was inevitable that the New Haven line should become as important a transportation link with New York as the Boston Post Road. The railroad was not the only way to go, but it was, for nearly one hundred years, the most convenient and inexpensive. Mount Vernon was the first of the commuter towns to take definite form. It was within forty minutes' ride of Manhattan. One-quarter acre building plots were available there in 1851 for $25 each. Twenty years later Mount Vernon had over 3,000 residents and was known as "one of the 'bedrooms' of the over-crowded metropolis." New Rochelle, nearby, has deeper roots in history than the railroad, but by the 1870s it, too, was advertised as a "desirable residence for that large class of active business men known as commuters." George M. Cohan, in fact, wrote an entire musical comedy about New Rochelle's link with New York, calling it, significantly, *Only Forty-Five Minutes from Broadway.*

If land was inexpensive, much more affordable than a similar parcel in the city, it was not necessarily rudely built upon. Williamsbridge, in the still-rural Bronx, was described in the 1870s as having "fine country places scattered upon the hillsides...one is often reminded of the city left behind by the displays of elegance and taste to be observed...." Wealth called forth wealth, and if it was forced by the growth of the city to move on, it jumped ahead further along the line—to Rye, Purchase, Greenwich, Stamford. "By means of the rapid transit afforded by this road," one travel commentator wrote in the 1870s, "the small localities along its line found themselves to be suburbs of the great city and much of the wealth accumulated in the metropolis has found investment [at Stamford] and at other places along the line of the road." Always following just behind the elite, however, were upper-middle-class businessmen who wanted a year-round residence in the "country" style, a bit of America where radicals and other pariahs with unpronounceable names were uncommon. The classic country towns of the area well suited these aims. If a village was not quite quaint enough, there were improvements that could be made—a country club for golf and tennis, perhaps a new or remodeled station, even a stylish parish church. The same writer who explained the move to Stamford reported of Cos Cob: "Some efforts are being made to change the preposterous name to one more high sounding...and more suitable for a growing and thriving place." In this effort the new suburbanites were defeated, but they succeeded in a much more important way—they gradually bought up the town. In time there were so many "respectable" residents that there was no need to change the town's name.

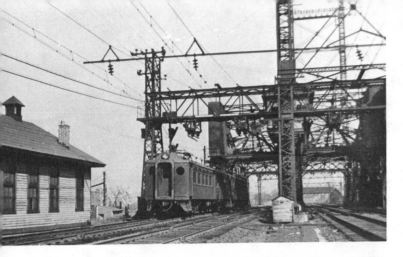

Above left, *Bronx River drawbridge, north of Westchester Avenue, the Bronx, New York City. New York, Westchester & Boston Railroad tracks are at left, and New Haven Railroad tracks at right, 1920s.* Above right, *electrified suburban train, New York, New Haven & Hartford Railroad, 1907.*

In 1872 the railroad was renamed the New York, New Haven & Hartford Railroad, a change reflecting the merger of the New York & New Haven with the Hartford & New Haven. In 1890 the little Stamford & New Canaan Railroad came under the control of the New Haven. Two years later the larger Housatonic system, including the Danbury & Norwalk, was absorbed. A Harlem River branch was also in operation for passengers in the 1890s. It left the joint Harlem and New Haven tracks at 129th Street and served the east Bronx and Pelham Manor before rejoining the New Haven main line at New Rochelle. In the early 1900s a subsidiary company, the New York, Westchester & Boston came into existence to serve White Plains on one branch line, and Larchmont, Mamaroneck, Harrison, and Rye on another. Electrified in 1912, the line was extended as far as Portchester in 1927.

New Canaan (Connecticut) Station, New York, New Haven & Hartford Railroad, 1940.

The South Orange, New Jersey, station in 1864 was a bustling center of early suburban life on the Morris & Essex. Sixteen miles from New York and ten from New-ark, the village was served by three daily "accommodation" or passenger trains in each direction.

The rural beauty of the villages comprising what is now a good part of the Bronx—West Farms, Kingsbridge, Morrisania—was graphically illustrated in 1878. Formerly part of Westchester County, the area was known as the "Annexed District" after being added to the city in 1874. A Hudson River Railroad train can be seen crossing Spuyten Duyvil Creek in the upper right-hand corner; below it is a panel showing the path and tracks of the Harlem River Railroad through Morrisania.

Jack tars from Larchmont, where there are fourteen yachts and twenty-eight thousand yachting caps.

Nutley, N. J., is the abode of genius. This is what future generations of commuters will look like.

The bearing of Orange society men toward other commuters.

Abnormal development of the eyes of commuters who travel through the tunnel.

All the Long Island commuters have gone into training since Sullivan went to Shinnecock Bay.

A quiet Mount Vernon whist party.

"Our Commuters" is the title of a group of comical sketches which appeared in *Truth*, a New York humor magazine, in 1892. Clockwise, from top left, the captions read: "Jack tars from Larchmont, where there are fourteen yachts and twenty-eight thousand yachting caps"; "Nutley, N.J., is the abode of genius. This is what future generations of commuters will look like"; "Abnormal development of the eyes of commuters who travel through the tunnel"; "A quiet Mount Vernon whist party"; "All the Long Island commuters have gone into training since Sullivan went to Shinnecock Bay"; "The bearing of Orange society men toward other commuters."

One of the last remnants of the golden age of commuting is private subscription car #3454 used on the Gladstone branch of the Erie-Lackawanna's Morristown line. The car is attached to the 7:57 each weekday morning at Gladstone, New Jersey, and returns home to the hunt country at 5:20 p.m. It is one of five remaining relics serving Conrail's Erie-Lackawanna and Jersey Central shore commuters.

The Lackawanna's passenger and ferry terminal in Hoboken, New Jersey, has national and state historical landmark status, and deservedly so. Presently used by Erie-Lackawanna commuters from many New Jersey and New York state towns, this weather-beaten survivor of the great age of railroad terminals is clad in copper and dates from 1905. Until 1967 it could be reached by ferries from Manhattan. Commuters to and from lower Manhattan have been able to use the adjoining PATH service since early in the twentieth century. Now both the ferry terminal and the approach to the station are filled with cars. Samuel Sloan, surveying the scene at left, would not have approved. An Irish immigrant, he rose to become president of the Hudson River Railroad (1855-1864) and then served as chief executive of the Delaware, Lackawanna & Western (1867-1899). More than any other individual, he was responsible for transforming the railroad from a limited coal carrier to a major transporter of freight and passengers. Restoration of the terminal, however, is expected to begin this year, and even Sloan may be restored to a position of dignity.

The "Pavonia" was one of two early steam ferryboats used to carry Erie Railroad passengers from Chambers Street in Manhattan to the terminal at Jersey City. In 1861 the railroad had tunneled through Bergen Hill and completed the new station. The ferry fare was then only 3¢. Within a few years, there were seventeen trains in service each way between Jersey City and Paterson.

"The Smoking Car," as sketched by James Daugherty in 1930, also provided a place for inveterate card players who retrieved their green baize board from a sympathetic conductor twice a day. Completing a game before the end of a run or an intermediate stop was a special challenge, and sometimes players had to be ousted from the quarters to face their business or domestic duties.

Below

In 1910 the Pennsylvania Railroad proudly published a sketch by Hughson Hawley of its monumental new facilities between Seventh and Eighth avenues and Thirty-first and Thirty-third streets. By linking Long Island and New Jersey to Manhattan through a complex system of tunnels, commuter traffic increased dramatically.

FRONT.

CASTLEWOOD. SOUTH EAST. ELEVATION   DAVIS. 1855.

72

Opposite

The Llewellyn Park section of West Orange, New Jersey, is one of the earliest planned country suburban developments in America, dating from the late 1850s. Families numbered thirty by 1870, and the usual building plot included at least five acres. Most of the homeowners were New York businessmen, as was the founder of the village, Llewellyn S. Haskell. Commuters could reach New York on the Morris & Essex via Orange. Later a more convenient station, Llewellyn, was established on the Erie's West Orange branch line.

Architect Alexander Jackson Davis was the designer of some of the villas which were handsomely sited along winding roads and the sloping terrain. Castlewood (below), was built for Joseph C. Howard and designed by Davis in 1857. There were alterations in the design, but the basic structure appears today as it did when proposed. The Gothic Revival cottage (above), designed by Davis in 1859 for Edward W. Nichols, was a modest but fashionable dwelling for a country gentleman's family. In form and detail it is very similar to Davis's design for a "Cottage-Villa in the Rural Gothic Style" illustrated in A. J. Downing's *The Architecture of Country Houses* and built in New Bedford, Massachusetts. Railroad companies were instrumental in popularizing picturesque country house plans, some of them derived from Downing's books.

By World War I the New Haven was serving a wide variety of suburban passengers: middle-class patrons of the lower Westchester rapid transit line; the stolid upper-middle-class businessmen of Stamford and New Rochelle; the elite country gentlemen of Purchase, Greenwich, and New Canaan. Stamford was still the formal terminus of service and would remain a key center even after the suburban wave had passed on to Westport, Greens Farms, Southport, and Fairfield in the years following World War II. Electrification of the suburban systems—as far as Stamford in 1907 and all the way to New Haven two years later—meant a considerable improvement in service and a steady increase in the number of passengers until the Depression years.

The eight-mile New Canaan branch (Stamford & New Canaan Railroad) was the earliest of the New York-area lines to be transformed from steam to electricity at the turn of the century. In addition to convenient express service to New York and back via Stamford, there were private club cars for some riders. The trips were made as comfortable as possible for these busy executives; even the conductors were noted for their clubby good cheer. F. A. Shute was one such friendly presence on the New Canaan Express each day. From the early 1900s until 1935, he ministered to the needs of his charges. Unbeknown to them, he also studied the manners and mores of the one thousand daily riders. Despite the exalted economic station of these commuters, it is doubtful that they differed greatly from those in other areas of the country. The conductor had his own way of sizing up a new recruit, to measure how well he would fit the local commuter mold:

> If he reached the station on time and in good humor; if he could manage a newspaper without getting it all mussed up and without too much waving of the arms in the process; if he refrained from talking to his fellow passengers when they were reading, working, or trying to sleep; if he could find his ticket without hunting through all his pockets; if he could sleep sitting upright and awake auto-

Snack bar car, New York, New Haven & Hartford Railroad, 1941.

matically just before reaching his destination; if he was perfectly shameless about the parcels he carried, feeling free to come into the train with a lawn mower, a watermelon, a scythe, an armful of roses or a statue of Winged Victory, I'd say to myself, "He'll do."

Novelist John Cheever could not have said it better.

By the 1930s the New Haven system extended from New York State throughout New England. In fact, it was overextended geographically and financially. Investments in electric interurban lines proved to be highly unprofitable. Operation of steamship lines inherited from the Old Colony, Boston & Providence, and other subsidiary railroads became a constant drain on limited resources. As New Haven historian John Weller has written, "The Depression was hard on all business but for railroads, with their heavy debt and operating 'leverage,' it was particularly severe." The New York, Westchester & Boston line, for instance, had never turned a profit and in 1935 was declared bankrupt. The whole New Haven system fell into the hands of trustees in the same year and would be run by them until 1947.

For the commuter the 1935-47 period was not all bad. Except for the Westchester line, the suburban system was kept basically intact in the New York-Connecticut area. New equipment was introduced to replace ancient wooden and early steel passengers cars. The creative sorts moving into Westport and Fairfield after the war—advertising men, artists, communications executives—were encouraged to make the New Haven part of their daily routine. From 1948 to 1950 the railroad even turned a profit. Unfortunately, this miracle could not be repeated for long. The number of riders had slowly declined since the late 1920s, and there just weren't enough new recruits to take their place.

Under the direction of President Patrick McGinnis and his cohorts, it is generally agreed, the New Haven was ruined for good. For three years, 1954 until early in '56, maintenance was sharply reduced. It was not all McGinnis's fault. Experiments with RDC Budd cars several years earlier were not especially successful; they were too light to trip the automatic grade-crossing signals. But by cutting back on routine maintenance in order to present a rosier short-term profit picture to the shareholders, McGinnis consigned the line to ruin. Even Wall Street knew better at the time and discounted much of the official New Haven pep talk and the profit figures. In 1955 a group of high-spirited commuters from the Madison Avenue advertising world sponsored an essay contest on the theme of "How New Haven Commuters Feel About the Railroad." The prize was a share of depressed New Haven stock.

McGinnis was forced out in 1956. In a bureaucratic shuffle typical of the time, he merely moved on to the Boston & Maine Railroad and there worked disasters similar to those suffered by the New Haven. In 1965 he was indicted for accepting kickbacks from suppliers. Meanwhile, there was new hope in the New Haven headquarters. In the late '50s *The New York Times* and *The New York Herald-Tribune* seemed to specialize in feature stories emphasizing the new look for commuters. What they were referring to were sixty diesel locomotives ($17,000,000 worth) which were to replace electric-powered engines. A corporate decision had been made to give up the then-inadequate Cos Cob generating station rather than to rebuild it. The cost of refitting the plant, however, would have been less than that of changing to diesel power. For this reason alone, the decision was indefensible. More important, maintenance of the existing system should have come first. But the railroad wanted a flashy new image, and the news reporters fell for the line. Within several years, investigators for the Connecticut Public Utilities Commission would find the graveyard of diesels at the Cedar Hill Yard. It was perhaps no wonder, then, that increasing numbers of riders in the 1960s should elect to travel what is surely one of the country's bleakest urban-suburban expressways, the Connecticut Turnpike, opened in 1958. Only in the 1970s, with state and federal assistance, did riders begin to return to the rails.

The Long Island Railroad

The Long Island Railroad has been America's greatest commuter line since the 1880s. It is by far the largest of the suburban systems and what it has not always maintained in service it has made up for in volume. Quantity not quality might have been an appropriate motto for the line during certain periods, but at least one can report that the Long Island has always performed its task of moving people at least as well as it transported potatoes from Suffolk County. If the glazed eyes of the commuter were sometimes mistaken for those of the tubers, the error was an innocent one. From its very beginning, the railroad transported people from the city to the country, and the economic and social development of the island is inextricably linked to the progress of the road.

Although the Long Island was not chartered until 1834, it can be said to have begun on its way in 1832 with the founding of the Brooklyn & Jamaica Railroad Co. The railroad's connection with Brooklyn is an historic one and was to be maintained in different forms over the years. The first steam ferries ran between Long Island and Manhattan in 1814, and Brooklyn was viewed, at least by New Yorkers, as suburban territory until late in the century. When the link between Brooklyn and Jamaica was completed in 1836, the Long Island rail corporation moved quickly to acquire the line and to build further east towards Hicksville. This destination, reached the following year, was named after the second president of the railroad,

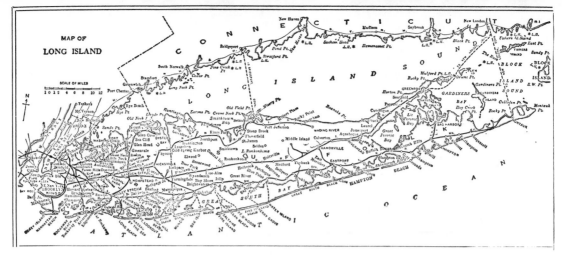

Long Island Railroad, 1936.

Valentine Hicks. The town, however, was only a way station to Greenport on the Sound, and the railroad attained this goal in 1844. The intention? To provide a quick (for the time) and efficient means of reaching southern New England with, of course, the additional help of the steamboat ferry. Almost from the time that the Connecticut coast was within reach, however, the New York & New Haven was pushing its tracks south to the city along the Connecticut shore, and through Westchester County, New York, to a link-up with the New York & Harlem. All was not lost by the Long Island in the battle for the New England market, but neither was much gained. There was, of course, the vast territory opened up by the railroad for settlement in the east-central section of the island. If a contemporary description of the land is to be trusted, however, the prospects of suburban development were none too encouraging: "the site of this road is through the most sterile and desolate parts of the island. After leaving Jamaica, you scarcely see a village or a farm of good land till you reach the terminus; but barren plains or forest of scrub oak, or stinted pine, environ the traveller on either hand. The principal villages, as well as the best land, are to be found on the sides of the island." To add insult to injury, the Nassau County farmers hated the iron horse and did what they could to sabotage its progress.

Residents of the North and South Shores, however, were not about to be left out of the railroad building business. At Flushing, in the northwest corner of the island, there was genuine enthusiasm for bringing the city closer to home. The area had long been a favorite retreat for Manhattan businessmen, a veritable early garden city of nurseries and suburban "cottages" which dwarfed in size most city dwellings. Located within only ten miles of Manhattan, Flushing was ready for the commuter just as soon as a railroad could be built. The Flushing Railroad was formed and began running in 1854. The first terminal was established at Hunter's Point, and two ferry boats were acquired for the crossing. Maspeth Village in Flushing had been launched a year earlier by speculators in anticipation of railroad service. A second group, incorporated as the West Flushing Land Co., started laying out home lots in the Corona section the same year, and the company built a station at 108th Street for the use of the villagers. On weekends by 1855, according to Long Island Railroad historian Vincent Seyfried, "special excursion trains carried prospective homeowners" to Corona, and they were "lured by the promotional literature of the speculators."

The early commutation rates were certainly reasonable—and commuters were treated with special care. The practice of setting lower rates for city businessmen was abolished briefly in 1862, and the resulting hue and cry is reminiscent of later suburban protests. "There is to be no commutation at all," the editor of the *Flushing Journal* wrote; "passengers will be upon an equality, and as democratic as democracy can make them. The commuters who are thus placed *hors de combat* were a most interesting class and will be missed. Their pleasantries, their growlings, their exclusive privileges of finding fault with everything that ran counter to their feelings for the time being—and all their agreeable and disagreeable peculiarities have been swept away at a jerk by the broom of reform." Reform, as always, was short-lived. Within two years the commuters were riding again at reduced fares and, of course, continued their complaining, as witness a letter to management in 1864:

> Why are the cars permitted to run day after day with windows broken, ventilators destroyed, with bell cord unhung, with brakes out of order, with floors unswept, with glass unwashed, and everything about them shabby and cheap?

Above left, *Jamaica (Long Island) Station, 1872;* above right, *Garden City (Long Island) Station, c. 1872-80. Both views are by G.B. Brainard.*

Several hundred commuters were traveling from Flushing to the city each day. When the College Point and Whitestone line (the Whitestone & Flushing Railroad) took over the Flushing Railroad in 1866, service improved greatly. Gas lighting was introduced in passenger cars in the early 1870s, and conductors were even dressed in uniforms from Brooks Brothers. Woodside assumed importance as the exchange point between the two Flushing lines. By the 1870s, hundreds of commuters had become thousands.

The Flushing area railroads were finally leased by the Long Island in 1876. Before that time, the Long Island had been using Hunter's Point as a terminus as well. In 1859, Brooklyn residents having convinced the New York legislature to ban steam locomotives from their streets, the Long Island had had no choice but to build a new Jamaica-Hunter's Point link and a terminal at the latter place. The Brooklyn area was not abandoned completely; an alternative teminal was built at Flatbush, but never again would it provide a principal way station for the island's commuters. In the 1870s Hunter's Point was also the end of the line for commuters using branch lines to other communities on the North Shore. Trains started running to the villages of College Point and Whitestone in the 1850s; Great Neck, Port Washington, and Manhasset were reached in the '60s. At the same time, the Long Island was extending a branch line northeast from Jamaica and Hicksville to Syosset, Woodbury, Huntington, and Northport; yet another was established to Glen Cove and later extended to Oyster Bay. After the Civil War, Jamaica station was earning its reputation as a major transfer point.

On the South Shore of the island similar activity had been stirred up in the 1860s by the South Side Railroad of Long Island (later renamed the Southern Railroad Co.). By the end of the decade it was running trains from Patchogue via Jamaica to a terminus at Williamsburg. In 1869 a second route, the Far Rockaway branch, was opened to serve this increasingly fashionable resort and estate area. After the consolidation with the Long Island in 1876, the South Side was rerouted to Hunter's Point. During the 1870s the first signs of commuter exclusivity appeared on the South Shore. Some privileged travelers could travel on rapid express trains made up of luxurious Pullman Palace cars. There was such service on trains to Babylon on what was to become known as the Montauk Division.

The last of the major independent lines to be built and finally acquired by the Long Island system was the Central Railroad of Long Island. The creation of the New York merchant Alexander T. Stewart who made millions from dry goods, the line was initially built as a way to reach his model village of Garden City. In 1869 Stewart purchased over 8,600 acres in the Hempstead Plains region for a new town to be designed for the urban middle class. The first "garden city" of its type in America, the village was to be linked by fast trains with New York offices and stores. It took several years to open up roads, landscape, and build model houses, and, of course, the tracks had to be laid. By 1874 weekend excursion trains were bringing prospective tenants for a "look-see". A contemporary description of the area helps to explain why it was not immediately the boom town Stewart had hoped for and why the villages on the North and South Shores had developed more rapidly as suburban settlements:

> There is some undulation in the country as far from the East River as Jamaica, to which point the Long Island road has run for many years, and this undulation produced a mild picturesqueness which is helped by occasional old farmhouses, unpainted and gambrel-roofed, and hurt by more frequent and more modern box-villas, staring in white paint and covered with mansards. But beyond Jamaica, the country subsides into the plain, and at 19 miles from Hunter's, Garden City happens, in the same casual way in which towns occur upon the great prairies, without any visible indication of nature why they should disturb at one point rather than at another the montonous equality of the landscape. There is a brick station and a brick "manager's office" adjoining it on one side of a square and a flat and almost treeless park, traversed by rectilinear roads, and decorated by two fountains kept diligently at play.

Prospective residents may not have been quite as affected by the landscape as this perceptive critic, but they were discouraged by one condition of settlement—A. T. Stewart was to own all the homes. When he died in 1876 and his railroad line was leased to the Long Island, few New Yorkers had subscribed to the idea of living in Garden City. Only after 1893, when individual ownership was allowed, did widespread building take place.

It was this center section of the island that the Long Island had first opened up in the 1840s. Railroad historians claim that the Long Island was responsible for the development of Mineola and, as noted, Hicksville. In 1854 a branch line was extended from Hicksville to Syosset; Locust Valley was reached in 1869 via Mineola. Farther out on the island's main line to Greenport were other early railroad towns—Deer Park, and Central Islip (Suffolk Station). By the 1880s Smithtown and St. James had been brought within reach of the Long Island system with the acquisition of the small Smithtown & Port Jefferson Railroad.

In 1898 when the towns of Queens County and the city of Brooklyn (Kings County) joined New York City, the Long Island had expanded as much as it ever would. Austin Corbin, who controlled the railroad from 1881 until his death in 1896, was an extraordinary manager and turned a profit every year. He was at home with all the influential New Yorkers of the day, many of whom carved out large estates during the 1880s and '90s—in Oyster Bay, out in St. James, around Hewlett and Lawrence—which were conveniently located for weekend living and, if desired, weekday commutation. The railroad's equipment was kept in good condition; the wooden passenger cars were painted a smart Tuscan red over which the railroad's name was lettered in gold. The Long Island was a first-class operation available to the commuter at economy rates.

After Corbin's death, the Long Island began its long descent into chaos. The suburban communities continued to grow, but the railroad had to be bailed out of bankruptcy by the Pennsylvania Railroad in 1900. The marriage between the two

New York City's Long Island Railroad stations, 1900.

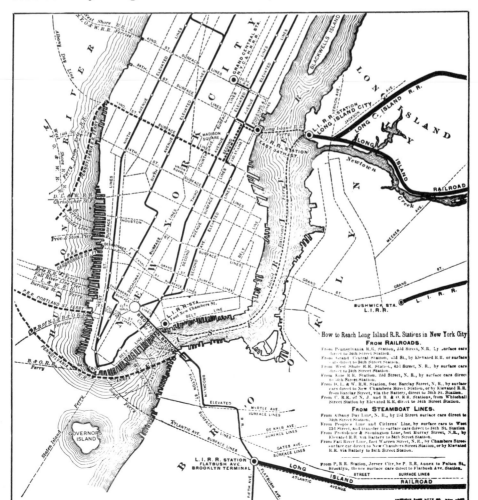

Malverne (Long Island) Station, and Malverne Estates Office, c. 1915, Long Island Railroad.

companies was a natural one in that both were still locked into their respective land areas and had to use ferries to reach Manhattan. The Long Island badly needed something more than ferry terminals at Chambers Street and 34th Street. By March, 1908, four tunnels had been completed under the East River which linked Long Island City (Hunter's Point) with the monumental Pennsylvania Station on Seventh Avenue. Electrified trains were first operated from the station in 1910. Electrification of the system had started in 1905 and over the years would be extended farther and farther east—funds permitting.

The new entry into Manhattan and modernization of equipment kept the Long Island on an even keel for some time. All of the wood passenger cars were relegated to the scrap heap in the 1920s. Throughout the first thirty years of the century the railroad promoted its suburban territory with special vigor. In a 1916 brochure entitled "Long Island and Real Life," no hyperbole was spared the prospective suburban home owner:

> Everywhere, inland or on the water, homes of Long Island range from simple cottages to formal estates which easily match many of the famous ones of the Old World—but all, mind you, *homes*. For Long Island goes in first for the comforts of life, and the gingerbread can come afterwards. It is well known, and will become still better known, for its home colonies, where building *en masse* and modern business methods have carried the art of living, for persons of moderate means, to very nearly its highest possibilities.

In case anyone missed the message, the piece ended with this appeal:

Great Neck (Long Island) Station, c. 1940, Long Island Railroad.

Why not know this friendly, charming place of great lawns, deep verandas, and country clubs brilliant and simple; of harbors and inlets that are a joy forever of yachtsmen; of model farms, oyster beds, and aeroplane schools; of Elizabethan cottages and French chateaux; of magical agricultural experiments under the wisdom of a great railroad whose story is the modern story of Long Island; of white beaches which sometimes, it is rumored, end in lovers' meetings, and of the old, old sea?

Why not know Long Island and real life?

Why not, indeed? Gatsby came and so did the briefcase-carrying, middle-class fellow later dubbed by the railroad "Dashing Dan," and used as its symbol. Some of the new suburbanites went only as far as Kew Gardens and commuted daily from the Richmond Hill station ("Fifteen minutes from Pennsylvania Station"). Others ventured farther out to Brentwood and Garden City. Nineteen twenty-nine was the peak year for passenger traffic; nearly 62% of the railroad commuters in America traveled on the Long Island during the '20s.

The rest of the Long Island story is less inspiring. Like every other railroad, it suffered through the Depression. Jamaica, always a confusing place, became no simpler a transfer point when the IND rapid transit line subway reached the station

Kew Gardens (Queens, New York City) Station, 1934, Long Island Railroad.

A 1935 cartoon by Rollin Kirby, The New York World-Telegram.

in 1940. Because of the way in which the railroad lines developed, nearly every commuter on Long Island had to change trains at Jamaica. In 1955, six years after the railroad once again descended into bankruptcy, A.C. Spectorsky described "the seventh circle of hell known as changing at Jamaica":

> People who have not done this will be skeptical. Standard operating procedure for someone taking a train to the North Shore, is to get on his train in the Pennsylvania Station, be carried to Jamaica, get out, walk across the platform, wait until a train pulls in, walk through this train to the next platform, walk across that platform, climb into the next train that heaves into position on this third track, and sit down, wondering whether the directions he received from the trainman back in his first train were correct.

It was all enough to make a grown man weep and to transform any number of rail commuters into travelers of the growing network of expressways. In the postwar period more and more businessmen and women, especially the recent newcomers, began to drive back and forth to work. The number of Long Island passengers dropped and dropped. A '50s joke was typical of the general attitude:

"Did you know that the Almighty built the LIRR?"
"Really?"
"Sure, the Bible says that He created all things that creepeth and crawleth."

Finally, in 1965, the state took over the railroad, and its politicians have rued the day since. It has been an albatross around their necks. Nelson Rockefeller vowed to make the Long Island the best railroad in the country, and like the Ancient Mariner, was becalmed in his plans many times. Compared to the sad days of the '50s, however, the present Metropolitan Transportation Authority operation is beneficent. When a proposed new upper East Side Manhattan station is opened, most Long Island commuters will be able to reach their homes much faster than riders in any other commuting territory.

The Delaware, Lackawanna & Western Railroad

To enter Hoboken's Lackawanna terminal today is to step back in time. It hardly seems possible that so much from the past remains intact: the graceful umbrella of a train shed, a concourse with an operable call board at the head of each track, an honest to goodness waiting room that despite its state of disrepair still has space and seating available for the traveler with time to spare. The ferry facilities—now used for parking automobiles—are still to be found to one side, a gently arching continuation of the main building. Bridges used to reach the boats are in place, and beyond them lies a clear view of the Hudson and the towers of Manhattan. The complex was completed in 1905, and three years later allowance was made for the entry of the Hudson & Manhattan tubes (PATH) alongside the station; this quicker way to cross the Hudson River from lower Manhattan eventually brought an end to ferry service. Now the copper-sheathed exterior is green with age, and interior spaces are encrusted with grime and peeling paint. But the trains are running, running well, and soon the building will receive the restoration it so deserves. Even now, however, there is not a depressing air about the place; instead there is a bustle and a spacious, hospitable feeling that comes only from a physical environment created not of synthetic plastics, but of raw materials made to last for generations.

In 1960 the Lackawanna merged with the Erie Railroad. A year earlier the Lackawanna petitioned the state of New Jersey to end all suburban service and was, of course, refused; again in 1966 there was an attempt to end the agony of deficit railroading, and several branches of the merged lines were dropped from service. These dramatic, overstated petitions to cease running trains did effect one important result—New Jersey started to subsidize commuter service in 1968, and, after 1975, all of it came under the jurisdiction of Conrail and the New Jersey Department of Transportation (NJDOT). Everyone realizes now that the subsidy program should have started much earlier. Instead, the state put all of its transportation dollars into highways and pollution. In this respect, New Jersey was by no means exceptional, but in the most densely populated state in the nation the effect was particularly toxic.

Delaware, Lackawanna & Western Railroad, 1936.

Hoboken Ferry, c. 1900, Delaware, Lackawanna & Western Railroad.

Lackawanna riders are now drawn from two lines—the electrified Morristown (with branches to Montclair and Gladstone) and the diesel-powered Boonton. Service has been reduced considerably from the peak periods of the 1920s and World War II, but it is still remarkably regular and frequent throughout the traditional territory. Maintenance of the trackage has been carefully supervised. It is not altogether surprising, then, that ridership has been rising in recent years. When new equipment is received for the electrified routes, there undoubtedly will be a further leap in the road's use by businessmen and women who cannot afford the time or expense of driving. For the time being, old Pullman multiple-unit (MU) cars are still being used on the busy Morristown line and its branches. These steel-bodied dinosaurs are in dismal shape, some with ripped seats and several coats of

Morris & Essex Railroad, 1866.

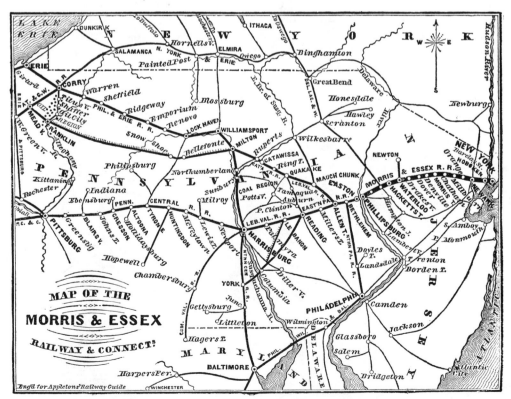

Montclair (New Jersey) Station, 1913, Delaware, Lackawanna & Western Railroad.

Maplewood (New Jersey) Station built in the 1860s and here photographed in the 1880s, Delaware, Lackawanna & Western Railroad.

The second Maplewood (New Jersey) Station, a Romanesque Revival building with fashionable timbered Gothic eaves, 1920s, Delaware, Lackawanna & Western Railroad.

Short Hills (New Jersey) Station, built and paid for by Stewart Hartshorne in the 1880s, Delaware, Lackawanna & Western Railroad.

peeling paint, but it is yet to be seen whether their modern replacements will prove as durable and efficient. Members of private subscription cars to Morristown and Gladstone would gladly forego the pleasure of the up-to-date equipment, for it will then be necessary to retire their especially-fitted cars which are now leased to them. The old wicker seats might be moved, but there could be no suitable replacement for the mahogany paneling. In any case, the public transportation authorities are not about to commission the building of prohibitively expensive special club cars, which no commuter organization could possibly afford to rent. The original cars were built in 1912, and are the oldest in service in the United States today.

Today's Erie-Lackawanna management is more concerned with the comfort and convenience of passengers than at any time in the railroad's history. The builders of the early Lackawanna were intent on hauling anthracite coal from Pennsylvania to the New York area. Only through the lease of the Morris & Essex Railroad in 1868 did the line of Phoebe Snow become famous in suburbia. The very first commuter service on this important division of the Lackawanna has been recounted in Part II, but there is more of interest to tell. The original Morris & Essex line extended from Morristown to Newark; by the 1860s it reached as far west as Phillipsburg on the Delaware. The company acquired the Newark & Bloomfield Railroad in 1868. Over the years this branch line provided an important route to Glen Ridge and to Montclair, the latter known before 1872 as West Bloomfield. It was, however, along the old main line of the Morris & Essex that suburbia first blossomed in New Jersey—in the Oranges and in Maplewood, Summit, Chatham, Madison, Convent Station, and Morristown.

Known for years as the Methodist & Episcopal because of a ban on Sunday service which the equally upright Lackawanna management continued from 1868 until 1899, the Morris & Essex cloaked its operations in the most respectable trappings of the area it served. The railroad might just as well have been given its nickname by the sabbatarian residents of Madison who, with the help of railroadman Daniel Drew, founded the university bearing his name in 1867, or by the righteous Episcopal establishment of Morristown, Llewellyn Park, and the Oranges. The gently rolling countryside of Essex and Morris counties held a special attraction for members of the Protestant aristocracy during the second half of the 19th century, and wherever they wished to stop, the train did also.

Llewellyn Park survives today as the earliest planned American suburban development. Tucked into a corner of West Orange, it was first advertised as being less than an hour away from New York by train and as an exclusive site providing "country homes for city people." Llewellyn S. Haskell, a real-estate speculator and drug importer from New York, bought forty acres along Eagle Rock cliff in 1853, and within several years possessed nearly ten times as much land, including fifty acres which were to form a central "private pleasure garden" for the use of the new community's home owners. The park and roads were to be maintained cooperatively. The Civil War slowed down the purchase of plots, one acre being the minimum, but by 1870 the overall property had been extended to 750 acres and the accomplished architect Alexander Jackson Davis had remodeled or provided designs for a number of homes. Haskell died in 1872 and the development of the land continued under the direction of his family and the interested aid of the first property owners. An 1874 publication sponsored by the Lackawanna, *Pen and Pencil Pictures on the Delaware, Lackawanna & Western* by Madison resident J. K. Hoyt, featured a map of the park and an illustration of the magnificent residence of O. D. Munn. The Lackawanna was used by the residents until a branch line of the Erie—the Watchung Railroad—was extended to West Orange in the 1880s with a stop at "Llewellyn" (Park Avenue).

The development of other Essex and Morris County communities was not quite as carefully controlled or imaginatively executed, but compared with what would come in the 20th century, these villages were models of good planning. They were also terribly Protestant, Waspish sorts of places until well in the 1900s. South Orange was described in 1871 as "a rural retreat for the businessmen of New York and Newark, and is the product mainly of the past twenty years." Of Morristown it was said: "Many of these residences erected by New York businessmen are very elegant and with fine surroundings." Impressario Otto Kahn was one of the Morristown millionaires. Short Hills was founded in 1879 by Stewart Hartshorne as a privileged residential sanctuary, and this land developer provided a site and $2,500 with which to erect the first station. In exchange for the gift, the Lackawanna inaugurated commuter service with two trains daily each way.

In the 1880s and '90s more and more of the land west of the Oranges was brought from what was then termed a "rude" state to a "civilized" one. Passenger traffic almost doubled from 1880 to 1890. Handsome stations replaced the first simple sheds. Glen Ridge residents boasted of their attractive new depot in 1887, the expense of which "has been borne partially by the railroad company and partly by a citizen, in this case, Mr. A. G. Dawson." Also introduced during this period were the express trains which carried the executive with incredible speed back and forth from New York. In 1883 "The Millionaire's Express" or, as it was sometimes called, "The Banker's Express," made the run from Hoboken to Morristown in fifty minutes with only one intermediate stop at Madison. Hamilton McK. Twombly of Madison was one of several wealthy businessmen along the Lackawanna with a private railroad siding projecting into his estate.

The Lackawanna further extended its suburban territory in 1882 when it leased the trackage of the Passaic & Delaware Railroad (known at various times as the New Jersey West line). This opened up an area in southern Morris County and in the Somerset Hills of Somerset County that is now served by the Gladstone branch line. Trains left the main Morristown line at Summit, traveling southwest through such villages as New Providence, Murray Hill, Millington, Basking Ridge, and Bernardsville. In 1890 this line was extended to Peapack and Gladstone. The timing could not have been better, for what the Oranges were to the wealthy

Gladstone (New Jersey) Station, 1899, Delaware, Lackawanna & Western Railroad.

Victorian-era businessman, the Somerset Hills were to become to his Edwardian son and modern-day grandson. Even the Essex Hunt Club moved to Somerset County. It was and is beautiful country, and as the Oranges and even Chatham, Montclair, and Morristown became more and more middle-class and crowded by elitist standards, the blue bloods tried to find a new hiding place. Gradually they moved west and south. As Louis Schlivek has written of similar developments elsewhere: "The houses tend to be baronial in both style and scale—it was not uncommon for them to contain fifty rooms or more—and with fine horses and carriages as standard equipment,..." In New Jersey the territory came to be referred to as the "three B's"—Bedminster, Bernardsville, and Bernards Township. In the 1970s this exurban area has become—thanks to the railroad and new interstate highways—undeniably suburban, and many of the once-large estates have provided perfect parcels for high-priced residential developments and corporate headquarters.

The far northern Lackawanna territory never developed quite such a fancy carriage trade. The Boonton branch was the result of the opening in 1870 of a new main line to Pennsylvania. It was to be used for freight only, with the southern Morris & Essex route reserved for passengers, but in the following year passenger service was added. Some of the new riders were affluent managers or owners of city businesses, but the majority were white-collar employees. There were always commuters on the Lackawanna and other suburban lines who lived in the country not because they wanted to, but because they had to for economic reasons. Simple pride, a *New York Daily Tribune* writer explained in 1901, prevented the secret city-lover from admitting his longing for an urban dwelling place. "He calls his Jersey home his country place, speaks of it as a sort of paradise on earth, and commiserates a chap for having to live in an apartment or flat in the city." In time many of these homesick city slickers lost their big-town ways and began to believe their own stories of suburban tranquility; their sons and daughters were stamped indelibly from the suburban mold and traveled to the city as children only to visit relatives or to shop. Inevitably, many took the place of their fathers as adult commuters. Among the daily Lackawanna riders on the Boonton line, the *New York Daily Tribune* writer noted, were "women, well dressed, good looking, and young. Their fingers are sometimes stained from typewriter ribbons. Women . . . always carry novels, and read every mile of the way. . . ."

In the early 1900s there were over 40,000 commuters passing through Hoboken each day. Lackawanna historian Thomas Taber, Jr., reports that from 1900 to 1915 there was an increase of approximately 80% in the overall ridership, the railroad's service having been made famous by the "Phoebe Snow" advertising campaign. Other railroads that passed through New Jersey could not report a figure higher than 40% for the same period. The Lackawanna burned anthracite coal until it was forced to turn over its supply of clean fuel to the federal government in World War I. Ships burning anthracite were much harder to spot by the enemy at sea. After the war, however, there was no return to the lily-white cleanliness of Phoebe Snow, and the railroad was to be dubbed instead "The Route of Old Black Joe." So much progress, however, was being made by the Lackawanna in elevating its main commuter line from Hoboken to Convent Station that the soot from soft coal could be ignored for awhile. By the late '20s, nevertheless, the need for electrification was obvious to everyone. In 1930 West Orange resident Thomas A. Edison helped to bring the first electric train from Hoboken to Montclair, and a year later the entire Morristown line, including the Gladstone branch, was finally electrified. The railroad thus entered the worst years of its life—bankruptcy, reorganization and continuing losses in the following forty years—in much better condition than its competitors. In 1930 the claim was made that the changeover to electric service (use of 3,000-volt direct current) meant that "the time of moving a commuter between his home and office has . . . been materially reduced. The average reduction is probably twenty per cent or more." The facts were not exaggerated. Further, it was predicted that the traffic through Hoboken, then set at 300 persons per minute during rush-hour periods, "will increase steadily. About one million two hundred and fifty thousand persons live in this sector of New Jersey, large portions of which are only sparsely populated." Of course, there was no increase; the Depression put a stop to it, as did the internal combustion engine. Today there are only 30,000 Erie-Lackawanna commuters. With new electrical equipment compatible with that used on Conrail trains, however, some service could be extended in the future to Pennsylvania Station.

The Erie Railroad

The Erie never intended to come to New Jersey at all. Its first operations in the 1840s began in New York State from a terminus at Piermont up the Hudson in Rockland County. Travelers from New York City wishing to travel as far west as Middletown in 1843 first had to steam up the river to Piermont some hours away. It was all rather silly, even at the time. There was another way to make the trip, and in 1848 a link-up was made with the Paterson & Hudson at Jersey City and its brother line, the Paterson & Ramapo connecting with the Erie line at Suffern, New York. By 1852, the Piermont connection had been given up entirely, except for freight service, and in the same year the two Jersey companies were leased by the Erie for many years to come. Marriage to the Erie was always a financially shaky affair and it did not bring either fame or fortune to the little New Jersey lines, but it did insure that Bergen and Passaic Counties would emerge as Erie commuter country from the 1850s on.

Looking back at the transportation history of northeast New Jersey, it often

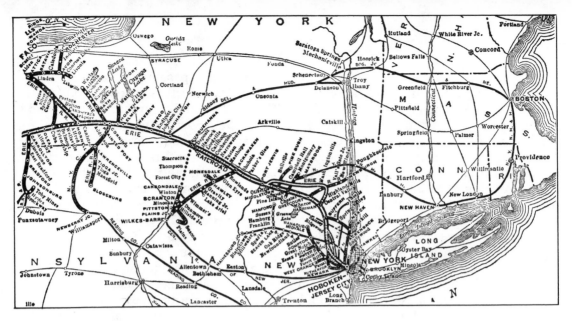

Erie Railroad, 1936.

seems that the early Erie management did little to encourage commutation— they simply took over local or regional routes which either fell on bad times or could not operate effectively without access to the Erie's main line—made up of the two Paterson lines—to Jersey City. By 1861 there was a handsome new Hudson River terminal and, miracle of miracles, a double-track tunnel through Bergen Hill which put the former Paterson & Hudson and the New Jersey Bergen Cut to shame. At the same time the Pavonia Ferry was established with service available to New York's Barclay, Canal, and Christopher Streets; later it also reached 23rd Street. The list of the suburban lines leased and ultimately absorbed by the Erie over the next forty years is no longer than that which could be compiled for other major lines such as the Long Island or New Haven. What is striking about the list is that all the small independent lines were operating within such a short distance from each other. They were the Northern Railroad of New Jersey and the New Jersey & New York Railroad, which itself included the Hackensack & New York Extension Railroad, all leased in 1869; the Bergen County Railroad, 1881; and the New York & Greenwood Lake Railroad which had already absorbed the Watchung Railroad, the Montclair Railroad, the Caldwell Railway Co., and the Roseland Railway by the time the Erie took it over in 1896.

The building of so many lines and branches in the second half of the 19th century is as good an indication as any of the intense commercial, industrial, and residential development of the area. When one speaks of the population density of New Jersey being greater than that of India, it is the northeast quarter of the state which should come to mind. Residential and commercial building, however, was fairly well spread out across the countryside. Except for Newark and, to a much lesser extent, Paterson and Jersey City, there were not cities to speak of, but only towns and villages. Hoboken, Montclair, Hackensack, East Orange, Elizabeth—these were to be viewed as urban centers only in the 1900s. In addition to these still suburban towns were hundreds of small villages which at various stages would become almost as closely linked to the Erie and the Jersey City terminal as the more established towns.

If the Erie was reluctant to lay down its own tracks, it was not backward in promoting the lines it leased and controlled. The first of these were, of course, the

Top, *Chambers Street Ferry Terminal, New York City, Erie Railroad;* center, *waiting room, Chambers Street Ferry Terminal;* bottom, *Erie Railroad ferry boat* Susquehanna, *at Chambers Street. All, 1906.*

two Paterson railroads. "Suburban Homes for City Business Men" was issued by the press of the Erie Railway Co. in 1867 and is a particularly intriguing early railroad promotional piece. Compiled by Henry T. Williams, later the author and publisher of books on household decoration and crafts, it included designs for suburban "cottages" along the lines of the plans published earlier by A. J. Downing, scenes of the countryside, and detailed information on the costs of "country life." Obviously paid for by the Erie, the pamphlet, the author insisted, was nonetheless an objective one:

> Within the last two or three years the writer had made it his duty to visit every railroad and station within a distance of from twenty-five and fifty miles of New York, for the purposes of obtaining information, as to what and how great were the suburbs of this great city, what were the conveniences of access, what were the natural advantages or disadvantages of every place, and where were the best localities for business men to choose their homes, and after a careful examination of the whole subject, I have no hesitation in stating, the greatest advantages and most conveniences are to be found on the line of the Erie Railway.

Considering the time, Mr. Williams may have been right. The Erie boasted of the lowest commutation fares in the New York area; the center of Manhattan's business district was then situated right across from the Jersey City waterfront and the Erie's terminal; real estate was cheaper on the New Jersey side than it was in comparable Long Island or Lower Westchester neighborhoods. In any case, Williams made it all sound very inviting, even the passage to the trains:

> From the City Hall, down Chambers Street, five minutes walk, takes us to the inviting entrance to Pavonia Ferry, the New York Depot of this road. The spacious boats Pavonia and Susquehanna, models of neatness, good taste, and beauty, are constantly plying across the river, teeming with the constant throng of passengers. Trips are made every fifteen minutes, to the Long Dock Depot at Jersey City, and connect with no less than seventeen local trains, each way, daily.

Ample evidence of the future of towns along the main line is provided in Williams's travelogue. Among the first of the areas to be encountered was Rutherfurd, now spelled Rutherford. A "Park Association" there was in the process of developing 300 acres and had erected the Rutherfurd Park Hotel to attract prospective home owners. Paterson was expanding to the north and also offering inducements for New Yorkers. "One hundred acres," Williams explained of the new section of town, "are now for sale at prices from $250 to $500 per acre. A depot will soon be built. A number of trains already stop here on signal." As was the case with other early commuter routes, the first stations were often little more than flag stops. As traffic was built up, civic-minded inhabitants made sure that their community was provided with a respectable depot, even if they had to help pay the cost.

The most inflated of Williams's praise was reserved for Ridgewood, or as it was then called, Godwinville:

> A New York business man can here find true contentment, and realize, if anywhere, his ideal of country life. It is really a happy scene....

The advantages were many—cheap building materials from the forests of Pennsylvania; a healthful, "salubrious" elevation; well-established stores and a conveniently situated station; and, perhaps most important, "In point of time Godwinville is easier of access than any place above Yonkers on the Hudson River, and in point of comfort of travel, far superior."

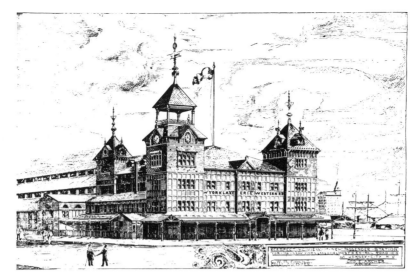

Perspective view of new passenger station, Erie Railroad, Jersey City, New Jersey, 1893.

Spring Valley (New York) Station, c. 1920, Erie Railroad.

In time the whole of the northern Passaic and Saddle River valleys would be filled in by suburbia, the territory closest to the New York State line being the most distant and exclusive. In 1886 the Erie opened a very handsome new terminal at Jersey City and was serving not only the communities along the main line, but those reached by the Northern, the New Jersey & New York, and the New York & Greenwood Lake railroads. Using the Erie terminal were commuters from the Montclair area; Hackensack, Oradell, Westwood, and Spring Valley on the New York & New Jersey; Leonia, Englewood, Tenafly, and Nyack on the Northern. Below Ridgefield on the Northern there was even a stop known as "Babbitt." Sinclair Lewis didn't spend too much time writing about commuters, but perhaps he did know something about the Erie's territory.

The suburban areas served by the Erie and its various subsidiaries developed tremendously during the 1880s and '90s, and no town was probably more important than Montclair and its subdivisions. The Lackawanna reached the town with a branch line in the 1860s, the Newark & Bloomfield. This did not, however, satisfy the needs of Montclair boosters, and in 1868 an independent Montclair Railway Co. was founded. This was quickly absorbed by the New York & Greenwood Lake, and, by the time the Erie controlled the latter line, service was well established to Watchung Avenue, Upper Montclair, Mountain Avenue, and Montclair Heights. Anyone who drives along Upper Mountain Avenue today will realize the extent to which the area became a sanctuary for the affluent New York businessman and his family. To some extent this crisscrossing of the town with convenient links to New York caused more development than was desired by many old residents. As is often the case, accessibility brought with it a host of new problems. The most important was to be felt acutely by the prosperous white majority in the post-Depression period. It is impossible to sympathize with such social concerns, to lament the loss of ethnic or racial enclaves. Montclair today is undoubtedly a better place to live for the vast majority of its residents. The large homes in some sections of the town which were abandoned by those who feared the loss of their prerogatives of class and color and were frightened by the economic decline of property values have been rediscovered by professional families from New York—black and white. Much the same story can be told of the Oranges which the Erie began serving through the lease of the Watchung Railroad (formerly part of the New York & Greenwood Lake) in 1896.

The Orange branch of the Erie was quite a fancy affair in the early days, and offered the commuter much better service than that available on the Lackawanna. The West Orange station featured walnut-panelled waiting rooms with fireplaces. As more and more of the area west of Newark became industrialized, however, greater attention was given by the Erie to freight than to passengers. Finally, in the reshuffling of service in the 1940s, this line, stopping also at Forest Hill and Bloomfield, was relegated to freight only, and buses—horror of horrors for old-time rail commuters—were substituted.

Tuxedo Park (New York) Station, c. 1915, Erie Railroad.

The remaining story of the Erie in suburbia is—as with the Lackawanna with which it was linked formally in 1960—one of slow but steady decline until the 1970s.

The loss of the Newark branch service to Belleville, Nutley, and other towns between Newark and Paterson in 1966 has been particularly missed. In 1956, four years before the merger, the Jersey City terminal was boarded up and Erie trains switched to the Lackawanna's Hoboken station. It was a sensible move, but nonetheless a regrettable one. Fortunately, service continues on the former New Jersey & New York tracks to Hackensack, Oradell, Westwood, Montvale, and Spring Valley; the route is known as the Pascack Valley Line and is part of the commuter rail service subsidized by the New Jersey Department of Transportation. So, too, is the Erie main line service to Passaic, Paterson, Hawthorne, Glen Rock, Ridgewood, Ho-Ho-Kus, Waldwick, Allendale, Ramsey, Mahwah, and Suffern. The once-proud link to exclusive Tuxedo and Harriman, New York, en route to Port Jervis, has been reduced to a mere shadow of its former self under contract with New York State's Metropolitan Transportation Authority. The little Bergen County Railroad survives as a useful link off the main line to the Fair Lawn and Radburn area which, since World War II, has provided new housing for middle-class families from the city.

 # The Central Railroad of New Jersey

While modern-day commuters on the venerable Morristown line of the Lackawanna are transported fairly rapidly to the city in vintage electric cars each day, the veterans of the Jersey Central's main line to the south through such ancient suburban towns as Plainfield, Westfield, and Bound Brook are content merely to wheeze their way to and from the city. Some of the cars are of the streamline-modern look last popular with the railroads in the 1950s; others are true odd-duck leftovers from defunct lines. All are the gift of the State of New Jersey's Department of Transportation which valiantly keeps the Jersey Central running between Newark and Phillipsburg for some 15,000 loyal passengers. It sometimes means an airless, steaming passage on a hot summer day or a chilling one in winter. Survivors of the Long Island's service of the 1950s and '60s will recognize the features of the ride: sudden lurching stops, the flickering of bare bulbs, clouds of dust arising from seats and window sills. It is all enough to make Our Lady of Liberty hide her lamp in shame. But it wasn't always this way, and, besides, there still is a glimmer of hope for the future along the route of this tarnished golden door to the west.

A rapid transit line linking up with the PATH at Newark has been proposed for the Newark-Plainfield "corridor." Whether it should use the Jersey Central tracks, or simply abandon them, is one controversial matter; a second concerns the terminus of the modern line. Plainfield has been targeted as the last stop. If the line reaches only this far, it will have attained a goal *first* achieved by the Jersey Central's wood-burning locomotives in 1839 when commutation was still an idea and not a reality. To make Plainfield, twenty-four rail miles from New York, the end of the line obviously does not make sense to the growing number of commuters who have made their homes in the area beyond. It is as if Conrail should terminate its Penn-Central main line runs at Rahway, leaving Metuchen, New Brunswick, and Princeton with only bus service. Skyrocketing oil prices should force a resolution to the dilemma within a few years.

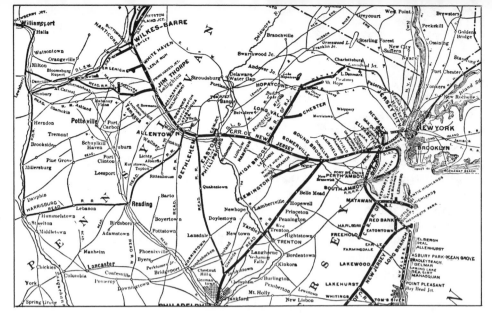

Central Railroad of New Jersey, 1957.

Plainfield—whatever the decision—will play its role in the suburban sun once again. The "Queen City" was once just that, the undisputed ruling sovereign of a handsome cluster of commuter communities. Gustav Kobbé wrote in 1881 of Plainfield's impressive Park Avenue homes, its notable families and cultural institutions including an art gallery housing an extraordinary collection of porcelains and cloisonné. "In few places outside of the great cities," he enthused, "can I have, as in Plainfield, a *sang-de-boeuf* crackle vase for a near neighbor, or be on a footing of intimacy with a cloisonné jardinière." John Taylor Johnson, president of the Jersey Central from 1849 to 1876, had made his home in Plainfield and he helped to set up the New Jersey Central Land Improvement Co. under the auspices of the railroad. In the years following the Civil War, residential development was very rapid, and special commuter trains of some comfort and ease were provided the new residents. The railroad thus profited from both increased ridership and land development.

While Plainfield and the area toward Somerville was the focus of real-estate agents' attention in the last several decades of the 1800s, Elizabeth, Roselle Park, Westfield, Cranford, and Fanwood-Scotch Plains won earlier acclaim. The railroad was associated with Elizabethtown, as Elizabeth was then called, from the very beginning of the line's existence. The Central Railroad of New Jersey received its corporate charter in 1849 and succeeded to the property of the Elizabethport & New York Ferry Co., dating from 1818; the Elizabethtown & Somerville Railroad Co., incorporated in 1831; and the Somerville and Easton Railroad Co., founded in 1847. Not until 1864 was the Jersey Central able to extend its eastern terminus from Elizabethport across Newark Bay to Bergen Point and on to a Jersey City terminal of its own. This provided the railroad with a much more rapid connection to Manhattan and a vital link for freight. Neither Elizabeth nor its port, now one city, were to be neglected in the move. According to a guidebook of the late 1860s, Elizabeth was "a favorite resort for many who, doing business in the city, desire a residence in the country." Contemporary prints convincingly illustrate the pleasant ambiance of this suburban outpost. The small city was also served by the New Jersey Railroad (predecessor of the Pennsylvania Railroad in the state) and was said to have "access to New York about every half hour during the day, and several times during the night."

Crossing Newark Bay from Bergen Point, New Jersey, 1890.

As Elizabeth prospered so did its satellite villages to the west in Union County. In 1854 the railroad's annual report stated that "The increase in the local passenger and freight business is very large…owing to the fact that the easterly end of the line is peopling with parties residing in the country with their families but doing business in New York." Some new residents were attracted to Fanwood or Netherwood by the rustic resort hotels and private clubs found there. Watchung mountain to the north and various picturesque spots for boating, fishing, and hiking in the area brought sightseers and numerous converts to what was termed the healthful "country life." As was the case in other suburban areas, rents were more modest than those in the city and, here, too, a city dweller might be able to afford his own house and land enough for a garden. To a much greater extent than was true elsewhere in suburban New Jersey, the towns along the Jersey Central developed as middle and upper-middle-class neighborhoods and not as enclaves of wealthy sporting types.

While Elizabethtown provided access to the villages of the west, its port was to assume more and more importance as a junction with the shore to the south. In the 1860s the Raritan & Delaware Bay Railway (later the New Jersey Southern) began serving Monmouth and Ocean Counties with a steamboat link to New York at Port Monmouth. In the early '70s the partially-completed Perth Amboy & Elizabethport joined the Jersey Central system along with the chartered but unbuilt New York &

Central Railroad of New Jersey Terminal, Jersey City, New Jersey, 1890.

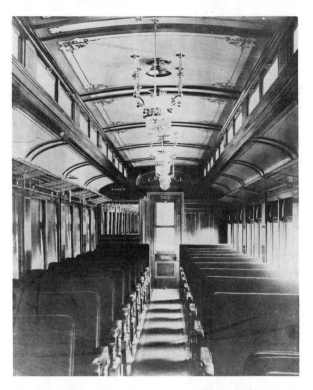

Lobby, Central Railroad of New Jersey Terminal, Jersey City, New Jersey, 1974.

Wooden coach built by Barney and Smith, Dayton, Ohio, c. 1890, for the Central Railroad of New Jersey.

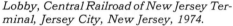

Long Branch. The Jersey Central completed both roads and thus established the first direct rail link between the shore and the New York area. The New Jersey Southern was bought out by the Jersey Central in 1879. By 1882 the new Jersey Central shore line reached as far as Bay Head Junction. A year later, an unusual arrangement designed to satisfy two competing interests in the Jersey shore area—those of the Jersey Central and the Pennsylvania railroads—was reached by which each shared in the operation of the New York & Long Branch rail system. It was a sensible arrangement that could have been wisely followed by other competing railroad companies of the day.

Why so much fuss about the shore in the 1860s and '70s? It can be explained in two words—Long Branch. This had become *the* resort community for New York and Philadelphia's fashionable families. During the 1860s steamboat service was available directly to Long Branch. The Jersey Southern attempted to meet the competition with its Port Monmouth rail and steamer link, and in 1865 provided a special branch connecting Eatontown and Long Branch. Long Branch, however, was just the beginning. Many other villages along the shore became favorite summer vacation spots. By the late '60s most ferryboat service was relocated to Sandy Hook, a better protected harbor and a shorter link with New York than Port Monmouth; there it would stay until the 1890s. In addition to its rail service from Jersey City via Elizabeth, the Jersey Central also established its own fleet of commercial passenger boats, and in the late '70s inaugurated the Sandy Hook Route for summer service. The steamers continued to be operated until World War II. In 1892 the boat-train terminal was moved from Sandy Hook to Atlantic Highlands as the United States

Army required use of the reservation at Sandy Hook for weapon testing. Although only seasonal, the Jersey Central's operation, as one writer has put it, "gave thousands of shore commuters, as well as trippers, a delightful ride through the bay after a hot day's work." The steamers received passengers at both a midtown Manhattan location and at the Battery.

The resort business was of primary interest to the railroads in the early years, but they also wanted to capture some of the year-round inland freight and passenger traffic which the New Jersey Southern had never begun to develop. Prominent among the founding fathers of the New York & Long Branch were residents of Red Bank, the area's principal commercial center. Through Red Bank a connection was established with Freehold, the Monmouth County seat; a branch line down from Mattawan to Freehold completed a circle of passenger service through the central area of the county.

By the early 1900s what had been resort country was slowly being converted to all-year use by New York businessmen. Philadelphians, who started the rage for Long Branch and its sister shore towns, were too far removed from the scene to take advantage of it beyond Labor Day. But New York was only half the distance away. Residential development took place both east and west of Red Bank—in the Colt's

New York & Long Branch Railroad, 1875.

The Monmouth *and the* Sandy Hook, *Central Railroad of New Jersey ("Sandy Hook Route"), at the Battery, New York City.*

Neck area near Freehold and in the Rumson-Fair Haven region—and was at first of the most exclusive sort. Private subscription club cars were the order of the day for commuting, and it is some sort of testimony to the resourcefulness and pocketbooks of the region's commuters that two of these vestigial remains of another age, the *Monmouth 2* and the *Jersey Shore Commuter Club,* still make their daily runs.

Some of today's riders may have inherited their seats from fathers or grandfathers who found such villages as Rumson, for example, awfully pleasant places to set down roots when the city was going to hell. In the 1890s Rumson played summer host to many illustrious gentlemen, including Jacob Schiff, the Kuhn, Loeb & Co. financier, and Cornelius Bliss, Secretary of the Interior in President McKinley's cabinet. What with the Rumson Country Club, an early site for outdoor polo, and the Seabright Lawn Tennis and Cricket Club, the oldest such institution in America, there were social opportunities aplenty for even those who chose not to sail on the Navesink River or along the shore. The rail connection with Red Bank was not difficult to reach most times of the year and, of course, in summer there were the steamboats to be enjoyed. "One reaches Rumson in eighty minutes from New York via steamer and rail," reads a real-estate brochure of the time, "by the most luxurious and fastest line of coast passenger steams in America, and the trip to Rumson is a pleasant recreation after a day in the office." It was if one could afford to leave the office early, and most did.

As late as the 1920s William H. Hintelman, a prominent local realtor, prepared brochures listing summer "cottages" for rent for the season:

> All cottages on this list are furnished complete, unless specifically described as unfurnished, with exception of blankets, linen and silver....Lessee maintains grounds unless otherwise stated.

At the same time residential building lots for year-round living were being offered. The Jacob Schiff estate was being broken up into several acre lots in 1929, and others followed in the 1930s. Even Rumson could not afford to be so exclusive in the Depression years as to maintain lavish country homes on a seasonal basis only. The same story can be told of Fair Haven, and of Middletown.

The saga of the New York & Long Branch since the '30s is similar to that

Red Bank (New Jersey) Station, 1890s, New York & Long Branch Railroad.

recounted of every other commuter railroad—decline and fall. The Jersey Central filed for reorganization under the federal bankruptcy statutes several times during the period. These were necessary moves but the drastic reductions in service by both Jersey Central and Pennsylvania trains were ill-timed. After World War II, Monmouth's still open acres were attracting more and more New Yorkers. In 1951, William H. Schmidt, writing in *Railroad Magazine,* spoke of "an increasing resident population along the sea, of the type which produces daily commuters." Since that time, the suburban stream to the south has turned into a flood. Hundreds of acres of farmland between the Garden State Parkway and Freehold have been subdivided for tract houses; trains from New York and Newark headed for Bay Head Junction each evening under the auspices of Conrail and the New Jersey Department of Transportation are stuffed with commuters who rarely even get a chance to acquire a suntan in their villages along the shore. For a time in the 1960s it appeared that suburban train service would come to a complete halt; now it can't begin to keep pace with the increase in patronage. Eventually service to Freehold may be restored, and perhaps even one day electrification of the main line will be effected below South Amboy, thus fulfilling a promise made years ago by the state. True rapid transit could give the Garden State Parkway a good run for its toll receipts.

The Pennsylvania Railroad

Service on the Pennsylvania's main line today is almost as efficient as it was during the early 1900s when New York was first reached directly via a Hudson River tunnel. Yet even before that time, the suburban towns along the path of the Pennsylvania's main line west prospered greatly because of their position on the principal route connecting New York, Philadelphia, Baltimore, and Washington. Over the years, the New York suburban territory has spread farther and farther

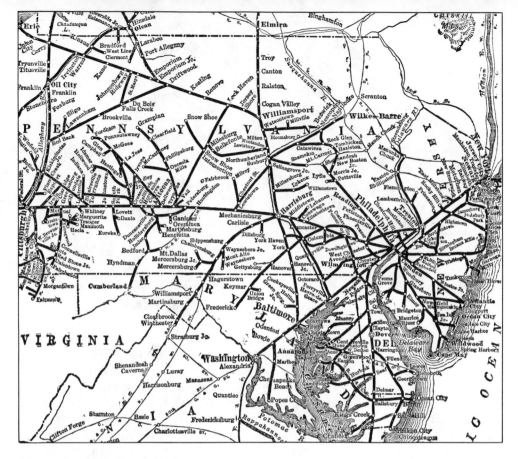

Pennsylvania Railroad, 1936.

southwest and now virtually encompasses the Trenton area—fifty-eight rail miles away—and adjoining towns in Bucks County, Pennsylvania. Commuters are even drawn from Philadelphia's western and northern suburbs as well as from the Quaker city itself.

The Pennsylvania did not come to New Jersey until 1871, but the tracks leading to the Jersey City waterfront from Philadelphia were already in place. The Camden & Amboy Railroad, designed to connect Camden, the small city across from Philadelphia, with South Amboy, began limited service in 1832 on its line running between Hightstown and Bordentown. The full extent of the route was completed in 1834; from South Amboy passengers could take a steamboat to New York. The line was controlled by the Stevens family of Hoboken, and a merger between the railroad and the Delaware & Raritan Canal Co., financed by Robert Stockton of Princeton and his father-in-law, John Potter, had been arranged in 1831. The two companies remained separate in operation but were one—the "Joint Companies" and later the United New Jersey Railroad and Canal Co.—in effective financial management. Thus it was only natural that the railroad line should pass considerably farther south of the canal which was to be built between Trenton and New Brunswick. By 1840, however, the basic orientation of the Trenton-New York main line had taken form, and the old Camden & Amboy route further to the south was downgraded. Stockton and the Stevens family bought a controlling interest in the Philadelphia & Trenton Railroad which connected those two cities. In order to reach the Hudson, a connection with the New Jersey Railroad was imperative.

In 1838 the Camden & Amboy started building a new line from Trenton through

Princeton and Kingston to New Brunswick, and the link-up was completed the following year three and a half miles from the New Jersey Railroad's Raritan River bridge. The New Jersey had reached New Brunswick in 1838, but had served Elizabeth as early as 1835 and Rahway a year later, and it had its eye on reaching Trenton itself without the help of the Camden & Amboy. The battles in the state legislature to win the right of way are legendary. Stockton, the more political of the two leading figures in the Joint Companies, was able to hold off this threat and, finally, in 1867 to merge the New Jersey Railroad into the larger combine. Three years earlier the road between Trenton and New Brunswick, which originally followed the Delaware & Raritan Canal as far as Kingston, had been rebuilt in more level and less circuitous territory to the south. This meant the cessation of service to the borough of Princeton, but with Stocktons and other prominent Princetonians directing the financial affairs of the railroad system, a branch to the main line (connecting at Princeton Junction) was immediately forthcoming. The Princeton Branch Railroad still operates today, a singular anomaly and historical curiosity.

It was the eastern region of the line—Newark, Elizabeth, Rahway, Metuchen, New Brunswick—that first attracted New Yorkers. Although Newark was not formally on the "main" line to Jersey City, the New Jersey Railroad had connected both cities in the 1830s. In the 1840s, according to historian Wheaton Lane, "The number of daily commuters became so large that for many years the conductors did not require tickets to be shown but accepted a nod from the passenger as a sign that he possessed a ticket." Eventually, wholesale cheating forced the New Jersey to add more conductors to police the line, and informality gave way to rigorous accounting. A yearly ticket from New Brunswick to New York, a special concession to the commuter, cost $65 in the mid-'40s, a figure that works out to about 10¢ a trip. There were also commuters on the Philadelphia & Trenton and the Camden & Amboy's New Jersey routes at the time, but most of these passengers were traveling in the direction of Philadelphia. Not until late in the 19th century were New York-bound businessmen likely to settle much farther west than New Brunswick.

Pennsylvania Railroad and Long Island Railroad lines in the New York area, 1910.

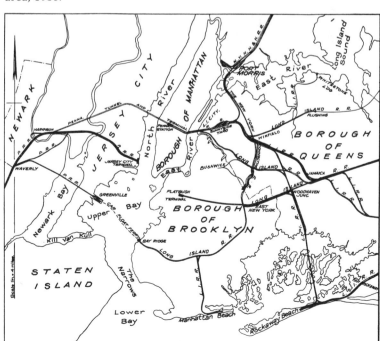

Commuters terminated or began their rail trip at Jersey City, and from there the New Jersey Railroad was well situated to provide ferry service to and from New York City's Cortlandt Street. In 1866 there were eleven trains in service to New Brunswick and fourteen to Rahway. Connections to Newark could be made almost every half hour from the Jersey City terminal. After the Pennsylvania absorbed the whole combine in 1871, passenger traffic flowed with increasing speed along the main line, and branch service to parts of Somerset and Monmouth counties came into existence. A handsome new Jersey City station was erected in 1874 and rebuilt after a fire in 1899. Slowly through the last few decades of the 1800s and well into the 20th century, this eastern section of the state became industrialized. When trains were first routed through the Hudson River tunnel to Pennsylvania Station in 1910, even the most hesitant prophet could have foretold the commercial and industrial development of the Jersey City to Rahway territory and its absorption into the New York economic market. The area to the west, still largely exurban in character— except for New Brunswick itself—began its suburban growth.

Vignette from stock certificate, Hudson & Manhattan Railroad, 1950.

Tunneling under the river had been proposed many times during the 19th century. Attempts at doing the job were made in the 1870s and given up as financially and technologically exhausting. By 1900, when the Pennsylvania had assumed control of the Long Island Railroad, it was imperative that the two lines be linked directly in Manhattan. Construction of "the New York Improvement and Tunnel Extension" began in 1903. By 1906 four tunnels had been completed under the East River to bring in Long Island trains; two years later two tunnels were finished for the Pennsylvania under the Hudson. Building of the monumental Pennsylvania Station was started in 1904 and New York's most elaborate railroad facility was opened for service in September of 1910. Before this time, however,

---

Opposite

The Brotherhood of Locomotive Engineers, founded in 1863, represented the most important of railroad employees who worked on the line and not in the office. This is William Arnold's "Record" and certifies that he was initiated into the brotherhood on January 31, 1881. Salaries for engineers were among the highest paid by the companies, and with good reason. The union is still an independent one.

Gravers Station, Chestnut Hill, Philadelphia, by Ranulph Bye, 1964. This exclusive suburban area was first directly connected with the city in 1854 when the Chestnut Hill Railroad was opened. Leased together with the Philadelphia, Germantown & Norristown Railroad by the Reading in 1870, the line was spruced up with extremely handsome stations. Frank Furness was Philadelphia's most noted Victorian architect and Gravers (also known as Gravers Lane), built in 1883, was one of the most successful designs for the Reading. The building now serves as a private residence.

Opposite
Wayne Station, Wayne, Pennsylvania, by Ranulph Bye, 1964. Waiting for the train in the post-World War II era—even a Main Line midday local—was not a comfortable experience, but it was likely to be a leisurely one. Wayne, some seventeen miles from Philadelphia, was founded in the 1870s by the publisher of the *Public Ledger,* George W. Childs, and A. J. Drexel. When asked why a suburban village had been established so far west, Drexel merely pointed out that it gave commuters sufficient time to peruse the *Ledger.*

Upsal Station, Germantown, Philadelphia, by Ranulph Bye, 1969. The Pennsylvania Railroad opened its Philadelphia, Germantown & Chestnut Hill line to rival that of the Reading in 1884, and this station probably dates from that period.

The Romanesque Revival style popularized by Henry Hobson Richardson was copied by station architects throughout the country in the late 1800s. Nowhere was Richardson's influence more strongly felt than in the Boston area—his home territory. The New Haven station in Stoughton, Massachusetts, was built in 1887-88 of granite quarried locally and designed by Charles Brigham. It originally served commuters on the Boston & Providence before that line was absorbed by the Old Colony and then the New Haven.

The firm which succeeded to Richardson's practice—Shepley, Rutan, and Coolidge—was responsible for the design of Newton's Boston & Albany station in the mid-1890s. The great sweeping platform structure is integrated with the main building and creates a horizontal massing of form which is typically Richardsonian. The station is viewed from under the Centre Street bridge in 1959, before it was demolished to make room for the Boston extension of the Massachusetts Turnpike.

A series of photographs of Chicago scenes published in 1907 provides colorful evidence of the handsome stations which dotted the downtown district and which earned the city its reputation as the railroad capital of the country. The neo-Romanesque Chicago & North Western depot, built in 1880, was then the oldest of the four illustrated. It was located on the site of the present Merchandise Mart at Wells and Kinzie streets. The low building closest to the Chicago River bridge is an annex which served suburban commuters. A new Canal Street station was built in 1911 to keep up with the large increase in traffic.

LaSalle Street Station was and still is the city's most conveniently located terminal for suburban businessmen working in the Loop. Rock Island trains to Englewood, Blue Island, and beyond to Joliet have used the station since its opening in 1903, and it is the only one of the four illustrated here still standing. Note the easy link to the elevated transit line.

At the south end of what was called Lake Front Park, the Illinois Central's main Chicago terminal was erected in 1893. Suburban trains continued on as far as Randolph Street. The new terminal was the railroad's contribution to the World's Columbian Exposition and it is said that over 100,000 people traveled from the station to the Hyde Park site each day.

Union Station, on Canal Street between Adams and Madison streets, was the eastern terminus for Chicago, Burlington & Quincy commuters on the east-west Aurora line. The station also served as a home for a majority of the Milwaukee Road commuters traveling to and from Elgin, Evanston, and the northwest. The building dates from 1881 and was replaced in 1925 by a Beaux Arts palace.

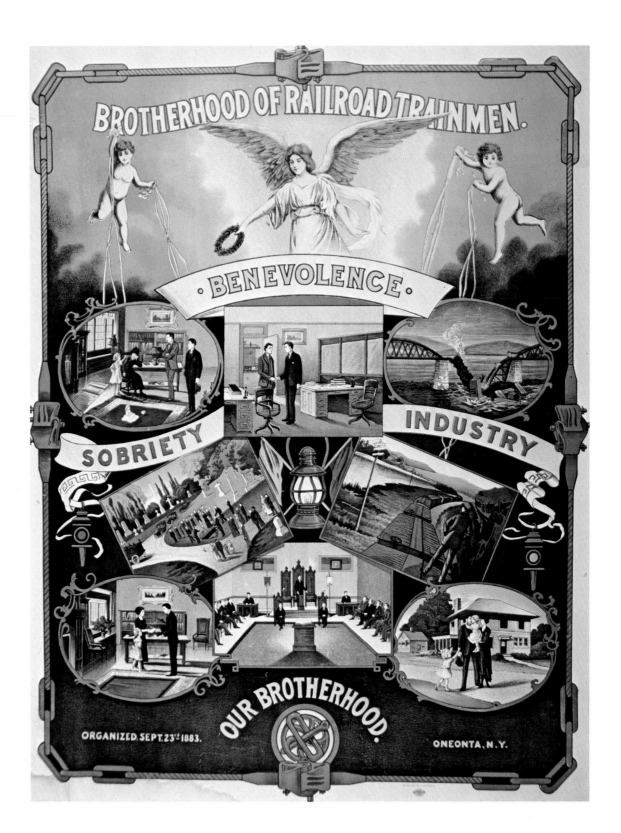

Pennsylvania passengers could take advantage of another tunnel link with the city—that begun in 1906 by the Hudson & Manhattan Railroad Co., the rapid transit predecessor to the PATH, and completed from Church and Cortlandt Streets to Jersey City in 1909. Two years later this rapid transit line was extended to Park Place, Newark, via Manhattan Transfer where a change between Pennsylvania trains and those of the Manhattan & Hudson could be made. Consequently, fewer and fewer Pennsylvania runs began from the old Jersey City terminal. The engines used from Pennsylvania Station were electric-powered and Manhattan Transfer also provided a place to switch from electricity to steam power until the whole New York Division of the Pennsylvania was electrified in 1933.

Pennsylvania Station and its miles of tunnels under Manhattan and the rivers brought both Long Island and New Jersey into much closer communication. A trip from the Newark area to the business centers of Queens and other eastern Long Island manufacturing towns was made feasible for the first time. In effect, the Pennsylvania Railroad substantially increased the extent of the operative range of the New York industrial market to both the east and west of Manhattan. All of this was accomplished long before automobile tunnels and bridges further enlarged the commercial circle.

The Pennsylvania's tunnels brought the commuter to his place of work and home again much more rapidly than did the old ferry service. Pennsylvania Station was intelligently designed and positioned to make maximum use of connections with Manhattan's subway system. Called a "monumental bridge over the tracks," the station designed by McKim, Mead and White, stood until 1963 as one of the last great urban rail centers in America. In a celebratory brochure issued by the railroad in 1910, the architects' intention is stated: "To express insofar as was practicable, with the unusual condition of tracks below the street surface and in spite of the absence of the conventional train shed, not only the exterior design of a great railway station in the generally accepted form, but also to give to the building the character of a monumental gateway and entrance to a great metropolis."

The last great leap forward in the Pennsylvania's development occurred in 1937 with the opening of a new station in Newark. With the suburban line electrified (and extension in the works as far south as Washington, D.C.), there was no longer any need to make a stop at Manhattan Transfer. An opportunity to link up the Manhattan & Hudson rapid transit service, Newark's buses and subway, and the Pennsylvania was too good to pass by, even during the Depression. The result was and is (in a now shabby way, although restoration is on its way), an Art Déco masterpiece in Indiana limestone. As the New Yorker's astute fictional observer of railroading, E. M. Frimbo, has written: "If anything finally does happen to Radio City Music Hall, we can move the Rockettes and those 'Rebecca of Sunnybrook

---

Opposite

The Brotherhood of Railroad Trainmen was organized in 1883 and was the last of four railroad workers' unions to be formed. The 1915 poster made graphically clear that sobriety and industry would be repaid by benevolence if misfortune should pay an unhappy visit on a widow and children. Considering the safety record of many early railroads—suburban and long distance trains included—such a fraternal order was clearly called for.

Farm' movies over here, and the customers will never know the difference."
Decorative plaster motifs and terra-cotta plaques are inset in the façade of the
building, and the main waiting room is a symphony in plaster ornamentation, satin-
finished aluminum, and ruby red Formica.

There was really little more that the Pennsylvania could do to make its service

Below left, *Pennsylvania Station concourse, New York
City, 1920s;* below right, *Pennsylvania Station, Newark,
New Jersey, 1937;* bottom, *electric locomotive of type used
in East River and Hudson tunnels, Pennsylvania Railroad,
1910.*

attractive to commuters — except to maintain it properly. In this respect, the line has been no different from others which had to suffer through the Depression years and the postwar build-up of the highway system. The Pennsylvania was, nevertheless, in much better financial condition to withstand these severe strains to its system and did not have to resort to drastic curtailment of service. The merger with the

Below left, *Princeton Junction (New Jersey) Station, Pennsylvania Railroad, c. 1870;* below right, *Princeton Junction Railroad, crossing Millstone River, Princeton, 1868.*

PENNSYLVANIA 3998

New York Central in the 1960s was thought to have been a wise economic move and in some ways did make sense. By the '70s, however, only the federal government in the guise of Conrail and support from the State of New Jersey could keep the suburban trains running.

There is little along the old main line now which will attract the attention of the sightseer or railroad buff. It has always been a rather businesslike route, and topographically it follows a path of least resistance across the flat Jersey mid-section. Southwest of New Brunswick is found the kind of land ideal for suburban subdivision, and suburbia has encamped en masse since World War II. Whole towns, such as Kendall Park, have sprung up where cows once grazed. On the east side of Princeton Junction, Walker-Gordon Dairy is no more, and area residents can no longer detect the pungent first odor of spring in the air. The Princeton Junction station is overloaded each morning with riders madly seeking a seat from the limited number available; the parking lot has grown larger and larger and more and more expensive. Yet there is still one symbol of the past to be seen—the quaint electric Princeton dinky, what some call the "Princeton Junction & Back," the two-car train of what was the Princeton Junction Railroad. It winds its way from the junction to a now shabby station on the edge of the university campus—a mere two and three-quarter miles. On a spring day it can be a glorious ride, and in summer a conductor may offer to sell you flowers or vegetables. Princeton undergraduates have been known to stage holdups of the passengers in true mock-Western style. In the days when Princeton businessmen with city interests traveled to board meetings only, it was a wonderful way to start and end a trip.

Philadelphia

Pennsylvania Railroad electric locomotive leaving Broad Street Station, Philadelphia, 1940s.

Behind the Times and Better for It

Speak to a New Yorker about the remarkable survival of commuter railroading in the Philadelphia area, and he'll mutter something like "They're just backward." If one is to equate the term "old fashioned" with "backward," then the New Yorker is correct; Philadelphians—and most Delaware Valley suburbanites consider themselves Philadelphians—are a most stubborn, tradition-bound breed. Thank God for them. Trolleys still run through the streets and to the outer fringes of the city; Reading Terminal, perennially threatened with demolition, with its market is still a beehive of rush-hour activity; Broad Street Station is gone, but commuters bound for the Main Line continue to descend to their trains a short distance from City Hall; and, miracle of miracles, businessmen from Haddonfield across the river in New Jersey can travel back and forth to work in 1979 faster than they did ten years ago.

In many ways Philadelphia is behind the times and better for it. Take the old Reading-Seashore Line, for example. If the city had allowed this service to the New Jersey commuter towns to lapse, if they had ripped up the lines (remember Los Angeles?), there would be no way to have created the high-speed Lindenwold-PATCO line in the early 1970s. At this time the need not only to retain but to rebuild the cost-efficient commuter-rail network (as versus the extremely wasteful auto-expressway system) was readily apparent. So few of the well-established urban-suburban links had been destroyed in the heyday of the internal-combustion engine that the job could still be done. In any case, Philadelphians have never been very fond of expressways. And now there is a fight on to prevent the construction of a Delaware River tunnel that would only serve to flood Center City with more cars and trucks. The old guard will probably defeat the plan.

To live in a suburban district rather than in the city is almost as old a Philadelphia tradition as the Liberty Bell. When the city was the capital of the country, the Fairmount Park area west of the Schuylkill and Germantown to the northwest afforded a place to relax and to breathe the fresh country air. While laborers were dropping like flies from the yellow fever epidemics of the 1790s, affluent merchants and politicians escaped—at least for the summer—to the healthful higher reaches. Much of the genteel culture they created—great Georgian homes and refined social institutions—remain to be viewed to this day. In the early decades of the 19th century, upper and lower Germantown, and to a lesser extent Chestnut Hill, became meccas of suburban life. It is not surprising, therefore, that among the first railroads to be built was the Philadelphia, Germantown & Norristown. Opened to Germantown in 1832, it was made a part of the Reading system in 1870. By the 1850s service to Germantown (and on to Norristown) was supplemented with a branch line to Chestnut Hill (originally the Chestnut Hill Railroad). Commuter service between these points and the city was well developed and by far the most extensive of the area, with as many as four rush-hour trains in each direction. In 1854 Germantown was politically absorbed by the city, an important first step in the process of urbanization that would slowly extend suburbia farther and farther away in every direction.

In the 20th century the Philadelphia commuter's life has been considered synonymous in the popular mind with that of the Main Line of the Pennsylvania Railroad, Kitty Foyle's territory so well etched by Christopher Morley in 1939. At an earlier time, however, the Main Line was barely known. Before Bryn Mawr even existed, for instance, prosperous city businessmen were moving northwest up Broad Street to Abington and Cheltenham townships, and the founding of the North Pennsylvania Railway in the late 1850s helped to keep the people coming. By the mid-'60s there was excellent rush-hour service from a Third Street depot to Fisher's Lane, Green Lane, Old York Road, Abington, and Fort Washington. A somewhat similar story can be told of the small towns served by the Reading on its main line to that city and Pottsville. It was during the 1850s that Conshohocken gained a reputation as a respectable "suburban" residential area. Across the river on the Main Line of the Pennsylvania Railroad, the real-estate business finally started to perk up in the 1870s and '80s. Suburban development farther south and west in lower Delaware and Chester counties was also a phenomenon of the post-Civil War period, and it was promoted by the predecessor of the Pennsylvania Railroad, the Philadelphia, Wilmington & Baltimore. To the northeast, the Holmesburg and Frankford sections had been pulled within purview of the city by mid-century; the classic country towns of Cornwell's, Bristol, and Tullytown were similarly linked at the time by the Camden & Amboy's Philadelphia & Trenton Railroad.

William Penn hoped that his city would become a "green countrie town," and he and his followers created as civil and as gracious an urban environment as would be found in 18th-century America. The civic leaders—they would be termed upper-middle-class gentlemen today—were mainly of conservative English, Welsh, or Scots stock. Many were Quakers or Anglican. Their aesthetic, though endowed by the Revolution with some democratic sensibility, was, nonetheless, Georgian and formal; in Philadelphia the Revolutionary era was codified by artists and architects in neo-classical form. When, by the 1840s and '50s, it appeared that Jacksonian and not Adamsesque democracy would carry the day in the city and the frontier, that the dream of civilized urban life was an impossible one to maintain in a city of increasing industrialization, many of the gentlemen retreated with their families to small villages where work could begin anew on a new social scale. They could at the same time, however, maintain their economic and cultural links to the city. In this way, they were very much like their Puritan brethren who kept moving their New England cultural artifacts farther and farther away from the city on the hill—Boston. The difference is that the Philadelphia sensibility was markedly Anglo-philistic. Two wars with the Mother Country had not unduly affected the filial devotion of the upper class, and the preference for things British has continued over the years. Suburban enclaves founded as late as the 1880s bear picturesque names reflecting not only the ethnic origins of the first settlers, but also an exclusive pride in family. Sprawling Tudor mansions and lodges, Cotswold-type cottages, and neo-Georgian residences rose in the pastoral valleys of Delaware, Montgomery, and lower Bucks counties from the 1890s on. Until World War I, and well into the 1940s, these were safe retreats for the prosperous and proper. And even in the 1970s the physical evidence of the genteel era is guarded with care by both the dwindling old guard and new arrivals who never had a gardener or an ancestor on the *Friendship*, Philadelphia's own *Mayflower*.

The Reading Lines

Although veteran riders and employees of the Pennsylvania Railroad will protest the claim, the Reading is to the Philadelphia area what the Boston & Maine is to Boston and the Long Island to New York—an institution of considerable age and shabby but noble lineage. Through sickness and health, the Reading has stayed wedded to serving the city. With branches stretching out through dozens of northern and northwestern Philadelphia suburban neighborhoods, it has never been far from home for generations of commuters. The railroad has not been particularly well since it lavished a fortune in the 1890s on its terminal at 10th and Market, and only through the aid of other lines did it make it to the post-World War II period. Now, of course, it is just another name from the past and coasts along on the largesse of Conrail and SEPTA, the Southeast Pennsylvania Transportation Authority.

Suburban commuters were not part of the picture in the very early years. As with the Lackawanna, coal was the gleam in the eyes of the financiers and stockholders.

The Reading was never to develop as spiffy a passenger fleet as that possessed by the route of Phoebe Snow, but it did begin to court passenger traffic over its main line west which was opened from Philadelphia to Reading in 1839. Just as the Lackawanna assumed the role of a suburban New Jersey carrier through the acquisition of the Morris & Essex in mid-century, so, too, did the Reading become a commuter line with the lease in 1870 of the Philadelphia, Germantown & Norristown Railroad founded in 1832, and of the Chestnut Hill Railroad. These two lines, merged in 1854, are not to be confused with the Philadelphia, Germantown & Chestnut Hill Railroad opened by the Pennsylvania in 1884. By the time the Pennsy's additional route was established, the Reading had been serving the area for many years and was moving to open up adjoining suburban territory.

The Reading continued to move ahead through acquisition. The year 1879 was an extremely important one, the key lease being that of the North Pennsylvania Railroad to Bethlehem. The North Penn first ran trains from downtown Philadelphia to the Lehigh Valley in 1857 and soon established branches to Doylestown as well as a New York branch which tied in with the Bound Brook & Delaware Railroad through New Jersey to New York. In 1879 the Reading also leased the Northeast Pennsylvania Railroad which ran to Hatboro from Philadelphia, and the Philadelphia, Newtown & New York which, despite its name, reached only as far as Newtown in Bucks County. The Newtown line had its own rail route out of northeast Philadelphia, but the Northeast Penn used the North Penn's tracks as far as Glenside. In the 1880s the Reading was as firmly entrenched in the northeast and northwest suburban territory as it was in the coal fields in Schuylkill, Carbon, and Northumberland counties. Perhaps this is one good reason why the railroad's fortunes began to decline after the '90s—passengers just didn't pay as well as freight, and there was to be less and less of that. The passengers, however, just kept coming in greater numbers.

They had arrived in Cheltenham Township to the north before the Reading took over the North Penn. Merchant prince John Wanamaker came in 1868 and proceeded —on fifty acres—to build not only "Lindenhurst" but his own private railroad station, Chelten Hills. At the same time financier Jay Cooke settled in, as did Peter

A six-car express train at Jenkintown, Pennsylvania, Reading Railroad, 1880s.

Reading bridge across the Delaware River at Yardley, Pennsylvania, 1882.

Arrel Brown Widener, and that early Philadelphia developer, William Lukens Elkins. He, too, paid for a station—Elkins Park. At least in the early years there wasn't a great deal that the railroad had to do to encourage riders. The North Penn's chief engineer was an astute fellow and reported to his superiors in 1854 that cheap, wooden structures would do for a while on the main line to Bethlehem:

> Private enterprise in a district so populous and wealthy as that traversed by your road will soon alter greatly the relative importance of different points, and I have no doubt that the first division [Bethlehem branch] will develop an amount of travel and trade that will astonish the most sanguine. . . . Until this development takes place it is impossible to determine the extent of accommodations which will ultimately be required at a particular station, and temporary stations will generally best meet the exigencies of the case.

How right he was. Men of the stature of Wanamaker and Elkins would do with nothing less than stone structures of dignity and strength and saw to it that they were built. Two of these stations still exist—Ogontz (called Old York Road in early timetables) and Glenside in the northwest corner of Cheltenham Township. Local legend has it that Wanamaker paid all the bills for at least one other station besides his own private stop—Meadowbrook on the New York branch of the North Penn.

It was not long before Widener, Elkins, and Wanamaker were joined by other wealthy city men in Cheltenham Township—Cyrus W. Curtis and George Horace Lorimer, publisher and editor, respectively, of the *Saturday Evening Post,* and John B. Stetson of the hat fortune. William Taylor Blake Roberts helped Widener and Elkins develop a 650-acre residential area in proximity to Glenside station. A thousand acres in the Chelten Hills neighborhood were bought and developed by Edward M. Davis after the Civil War. With this kind of start in the 1860s and '70s, there was no end in sight to the possibilities of residential development. A rapid transit trolley line, the Union Traction Co., controlled by Widener and Elkins, arrived in the township in 1895, and this service ushered in a new suburban age, a second stage of expansion suited to the needs of those of more modest means.

Homes costing $19,000 each were built in the Latham Park area in 1912. Expensive for the time, they were not, however, of the baronial proportions required by the wealthy Victorians. Elkins Park was by now very "smart" and attracted more and more of the respectable upper middle class who had watched their North Philadelphia neighborhoods decline with industrialization. After World War I, successful German-Jewish businessmen found the area an accessible and pleasant sanctuary from the city. During the Depression the influx of Jewish families grew as the large early estates were broken up into good-sized but manageable lots. It was then, too, that barriers of prejudice began to fall in the area to the north, Abington Township. The cultural life of the Abington-Cheltenham communities—Elkins Park, Melrose Park, La Mott, Cheltenham, Jenkintown, Glenside, Noble, Abington, Rydal—was considerably enriched by the arrival of professional and economically-successful Jewish families. That the area's tradition of religious tolerance, institutionalized in the several Quaker meetings, provided an intellectual and social climate much more welcoming and open than that prevailing in other upper-class towns is unquestionable.

Cheltenham Township was, however, right on the border of the city, and this proximity was to test its welcoming spirit for many years to come. By the 1880s, the area was not far enough away from Philadelphia for many who sought seclusion and the real country life. They could travel farther up the Bethlehem line, branch off toward Doylestown, or from Jenkintown, follow the New York branch through Rydal, Meadowbrook, and Bethayres toward Yardley and West Trenton. For a Philadelphia-area businessman called upon to make frequent trips to New York, this was an ideal route to ride. As late as 1930 he could climb aboard the train at Meadowbrook at 7:50 a.m. and arrive in New York via the Reading's New Jersey connections (including the Jersey Central ferry at Jersey City) at 10:12 a.m. The return trip could be made with similar speed and ease. If the villages along this New York branch did not appeal to the prospective suburbanite, there was always the Newtown branch to be explored. It did not offer as convenient a link to New York for the executive, but it did provide a speedy route to Philadelphia and back which took the commuter through the lush green countryside of eastern Cheltenham Township, Fox Chase, Huntingdon Valley, Bryn Athyn, and, farther afield, the Newtown area of prosperous Quaker farms and handsome stone farmhouses.

In the early 1900s more and more of Philadelphia's successful families sought out the quiet of lower Bucks County. The extension of the Reading's Northeast Pennsylvania Railroad from Hatboro to Ivyland and on to New Hope in 1891 had made access much easier for the commuter. While many homes were only country

Top, *Ivyland (Pennsylvania) Station, 1940;* bottom, *Boycot (Pennsylvania) Station, 1940, built for Judge Edward M. Paxson. Both, New Hope Branch, Reading Railroad (North East Pennsylvania Railroad).*

Philadelphia & Reading Railroad Depot, Philadelphia, 1882.

places for the weekend, the very fact that one could travel to and from the city by train made a residence in this exurban territory more attractive. As was done years earlier in Cheltenham Township, private stations were built. Most of these were only flag stops with a picturesque shelter. Today the Ivyland to New Hope extension is no longer in service except as a short-haul carrier of freight and excursion railroaders. Suburbia did not reach out into the area until the late 1940s, and by this time it was too late to save the line. Now, of course, the countryside is filling up with the homes of Philadelphia-area families who must drive to Doylestown or Newtown if they are to commute to the city by rail.

Until 1893 commuters on the Reading's North Penn branches, the North East Penn, and the Philadelphia, Germantown & Norristown used a station at 9th and Green Streets in Philadelphia, while main line Reading trains entered and left a terminal at Callowhill and Broad Streets. An extremely handsome granite-faced building in the Italian-Renaissance style brought all the lines together at one convenient location. The train shed, a single span of 256 feet, was a singular engineering achievement at the time and remains a landmark today. Trains depart on an upper level, and below them sprawls the famous farmer's market. Most of the railroad's offices are gone now from the building, and the public spaces have become badly marred by the neglect of maintenance. Just what will happen to the building is uncertain as Conrail seeks to fashion an affordable and efficient transportation system. The Reading Terminal, however, could once again serve as a multipurpose transportation "center," offering commuters not only convenient access to the city's business center but also the amenities of shops and restaurants.

Reading Terminal, Philadelphia, 1893.

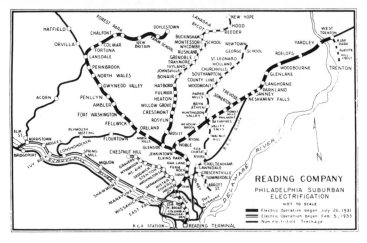

Suburban electrification, Reading Co., 1963.

Boston's resuscitated Quincy Market and Faneuil Hall complex, as successful as it is, still exists as a somewhat isolated island and serves no immediate practical purpose. Reading Terminal, a most functional complex, serves a purpose which even a computer programmer of the 1970s can systematically understand.

Electrification of most of the Reading's suburban territory in the late 1920s and early '30s resulted in an increase in ridership during a period when most railroads reported only losses. The running time between Center City and the suburbs was considerably improved by the use of equipment which could accelerate much more rapidly after stops than the steam locomotives they replaced. The first multiple-unit cars, are, of course, terribly worn now, but they are being replaced by more modern equipment. The commuters on the Reading, like those of the Lackawanna's Morristown line, only hope that the car builders of today are as skilled as those of the 1920s.

The Pennsylvania Railroad

The eminently respectable Pennsylvania of 20th-century fame was a Johnny-come-lately on the Philadelphia suburban scene; even the traditional "Paoli Local," as any historically-minded Reading commuter will remind you, started running years later than the trains to Germantown and Chestnut Hill. As an operating railroad company, the Pennsylvania dates from 1853, but not until twenty years later did development begin along the railroad's main route to the west. In the 1880s the Pennsy came into its own as a major Philadelphia suburban carrier. At this time it controlled the Philadelphia, Wilmington & Baltimore Railroad route to the south, and the United New Jersey Railroad and Canal Co. lines (consisting of the Camden & Amboy, Philadelphia & Trenton, and New Jersey railroads) to the northeast, and had, in 1884, entered into direct competition with the Reading for passenger traffic to Germantown and Chestnut Hill. And it had the resources to develop its Main Line territory.

The Pennsylvania corporation, merged with the New York Central in the 1960s, still exists and in recent years has turned handsome profits. Passenger service, however, is no longer its responsibility or interest. Suburban service is now directed by Conrail under contract with the Southeastern Pennsylvania Transportation

Authority, an arrangement also shared with the Reading. To most riders, it's still the same old Pennsy nonetheless, and the trains are running just about as well as they did fifty years ago when railroad commuting was taken for granted. There are fewer trains, but there are also fewer riders than in the 1920s. If gasoline continues in short supply (and what other prospect is there?), then the Pennsylvania's all-electric fleet may have to be expanded.

The Pennsylvania became an octopus in the late 19th century, reaching out in every possible direction for riders and freight. There is no doubt that the company overextended itself, but, unlike the creature of Frank Norris's novel, the Pennsylvania fed rather than bled Philadelphia's suburban territory. The history of the residential

Passenger depots, Philadelphia, Germantown & Chestnut Hill Railroad, 1893. Clockwise: *Queen's Lane, Chelton Avenue, Wissihickon, Chestnut Hill;* center, *Chelton Avenue.*

Main Line, Pennsylvania Railroad, Southeast Pennsylvania Transportation Authority and Conrail, 1979.

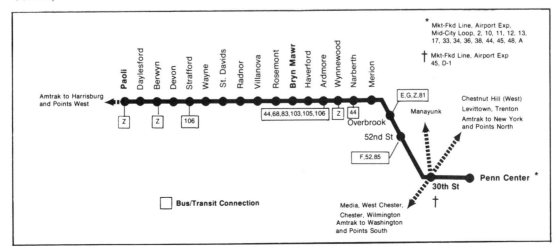

villages on the Main Line provides an instructive case in point. When the company gained rights to the trackage of the state-financed Philadelphia & Columbia Railroad in the 1850s, a small handful of farmers and mechanics lived in such settlements on the way to Paoli as Whitehall, Morgan's Corners, and Eagle. These were stops on the Philadelphia division of the Pennsylvania in the 1860s. By the mid-1870s, Whitehall was known as Rosemont, Morgan's Corners as Radnor, and Eagle was on the way to becoming Devon, all three having acquired "tonier" names. During the same period, Overbrook, Merion, Wynnewood, Ardmore, Haverford, Bryn Mawr, Villanova, St. David's, and Wayne were added to the schedule of stops. This was only a beginning of service to a string of expanding and extremely affluent communities that in time would symbolize to the outsider everything that was attractive and romantic, snobbish and illiberal about suburbia.

In the late 1860s the tracks west were realigned in the Whitehall area, and, in order to expedite the work, it was necessary to buy up a number of large parcels of land. Thus began the settlement of Bryn Mawr. The unincorporated town was named by the railroad after the home of Rowland Ellis, a colonial settler who had proudly acknowledged his Welsh ancestral roots. Within a short time of its founding, Bryn Mawr was also the name extended to the village of Humphreysville on the old Lancaster Pike. It was only natural that the Pennsylvania should seek to develop much of its land for residential purposes. Like the management of such early railroad companies as the New York & Harlem and the Jersey Central, the Pennsylvania executives decided that a hotel should be built to attract future residents; at first, there would be an opportunity for weekend excursions to the country. The area already had summer residents, not a great many but enough to fill up a few boarding houses. In 1874 a prospectus issued by the railroad gave the names of fifty-four boarding houses located from Overbrook to Downington which would house as many as 1,330 summer guests. The Bryn Mawr Hotel, with room for eighty was, of course, prominently featured. It was no small matter of pride that Bryn Mawr's elevation of over 400 feet placed it not only above that of steamy Philadelphia, but at least four inches higher than that of socially prominent Chestnut Hill.

According to a history of the Main Line privately published in 1922, the Bryn Mawr Hotel in the 1880s "became a favorite resort for men who could not leave their business for more than the conventional two weeks in summer, and wives were content then to stay with their husbands near the source of their revenue." This chronicler of the good old days, J. W. Townsend, remembered them well and could not refrain from dropping names:

> Among those at the Bryn Mawr Hotel were P.R.R.'s Vice President, Mr. Du Barry, and his family, and Vice President Cassatt's parents and artist sister. The elder Mr. Cassatt was a 'gentleman of the old school,' tall and dignified, dressed in summer in an immaculately clean white linen suit.

The listing of the squirearchy went on and on. Some, as the above, were associated with the railroad; nearly all were stockholders of some prominence. Eventually a good number of them decided that life in the country was a great deal more pleasant than that in the city and settled down for more than a summer. These first permanent settlers attracted more and more of their own kind. It wasn't easy to lay down roots; no house was to cost less than $5,000, (at a time when $500 could buy five acres and a house in the sticks), and those on Montgomery Avenue in Bryn Mawr, the railroad decreed, were to be built at a starting price of $8,000. "Buildings for any offensive occupation" were effectively barred, and this included any sort of

Bryn Mawr (Pennsylvania) Station, Pennsylvania Railroad, 1963.

manufacturing or other commercial venture. With the establishment of Bryn Mawr College for women in 1885, the village was given exactly what the railroad's managers desired—a respectable, institutional tone of permanent class.

Until the 1930s the Main Line spread farther and farther west as an exclusive chain of upper-class neighborhoods. George W. Childs, editor of *The Public Ledger,* settled in Bryn Mawr in the late '60s and then moved on to found (with A. J. Drexel)

Broad Street Station, Philadelphia, Pennsylvania Railroad, 1893.

the village of Wayne. Naturally they changed its original name from Louella to honor gentleman farmer and Revolutionary hero "Mad Anthony Wayne" whose manor house was located in the Paoli area. Also responsible for developing the Main Line was Owen Jones, a real-estate operator best remembered for his adage that land should be "purchased by the acre but sold by the foot." Unfortunately, his advice has been followed too rigorously by modern-day speculators for the good of the area. Before the Depression and until income taxes bit in heavily, however, Main Line towns from Merion to Paoli were, in the words of Main Line historian Townsend, part of a "vast garden." Writing in 1922, he was particularly proud of the work of the gentleman farmers who "subjectively improve themselves" by doing the work of laborers in the fields. These city executives had to stretch their muscles because even in this Eden, "The dagoes, bless them, [are] getting any price they choose to ask for their labor, when it is scarce," as it was at the time. These words were written in the same year that *Babbitt* was published.

Since that time families decidely not "old Main Line" have made the area into a much more democratic enviroment in both the political and social meaning of the phrase. The railroad, of course, made it possible for many more families to enjoy the suburban territory, and they have profited from the service offered by the Pennsylvania. Electrification as far west as Paoli in 1915 resulted in faster trips to even the most secluded little valleys. In defense of the Main Line's *ancien régime*, however, it is only right to repeat historian Townsend's remarks on the tradition of railroad commuting first established by the wealthy early commuters: "They use the trains and trolleys, and have no limousines to block the city's narrow streets or to require a wide Parkway for the journey to and fro." The Schuylkill Expressway arrived in time, but no respectable Main Liner—new or old—really likes to use it.

While the Pennsylvania was vigorously promoting its western territory, commuters were also beginning to use lines to the east and north of the city. A link (the Connecting Railway) between the main route and the Philadelphia & Trenton Railroad was built in 1867 from Mantua to Frankford Junction. In addition to establishing a new and faster east-west route to New York City, the branch brought North Philadelphia and the eastern portion of lower Bucks County into much closer communication with the city. In 1879 a Center City station was needed to house both general offices and the rapidly increasing numbers of trains and passengers heading in various directions. Broad Street Station became a reality in 1881; by 1894 it had to be expanded considerably.

When Broad Street Station first opened, the daily passenger trains of the Philadelphia, Wilmington & Baltimore Railroad were added to those of the Pennsylvania. This line had been acquired earlier in the year, and with it came 330 miles of trackage, including commuter lines to West Chester and Chester. The P.W. & B. provided an important southern connection with the Pennsylvania-controlled Baltimore & Potomac Railroad. With the merger of these two lines, the Philadelphia, Baltimore & Washington Railroad came into being to challenge the Baltimore & Ohio for intercity traffic. In the 1880s only the New York Central system could rival that of the Pennsylvania; by 1910, with the completion of a magnificent station in New York, the Pennsylvania was undoubtedly the leader in American transportation. It then controlled the Long Island Railroad and a network of New Jersey and Pennsylvania commuter lines (and additional suburban service in Pittsburgh, Washington, Cleveland, Baltimore, and Chicago). The Pennsylvania was also the winner in short-haul passenger traffic.

The Philadelphia, Wilmington & Baltimore was one of the best acquisitions.

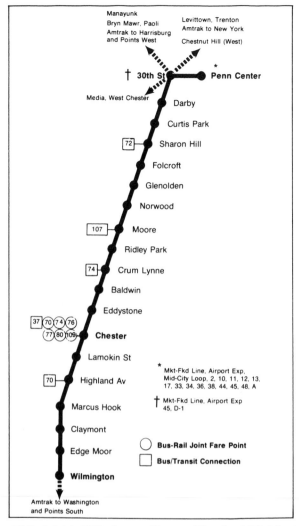

Inside the figure:

Manayunk
Bryn Mawr, Paoli
Amtrak to Harrisburg
and Points West

Levittown, Trenton
Amtrak to New York

Chestnut Hill (West)

† 30th St   * Penn Center

Media, West Chester

Darby

Curtis Park

72   Sharon Hill

Folcroft

Glenolden

Norwood

107   Moore

Ridley Park

74   Crum Lynne

Baldwin

Eddystone

37 70 74 76
77 80 109   Chester

Lamokin St

*
Mkt-Fkd Line, Airport Exp,
Mid-City Loop, 2, 10, 11, 12, 13,
17, 33, 34, 36, 38, 44, 45, 48, A

70   Highland Av

† Mkt-Fkd Line, Airport Exp
45, D-1

Marcus Hook

Claymont

Edge Moor

◯ **Bus-Rail Joint Fare Point**

▢ **Bus/Transit Connection**

Wilmington

Amtrak to Washington
and Points South

*Philadelphia-Wilmington (former Maryland Division)
line, Pennsylvania Railroad, Southeast Pennsylvania
Transportation Authority and Conrail, 1979.*

Founded in 1830, it offered suburban and intercity service long before the Pennsylvania existed. Its first and only Philadelphia station was located at Broad Street and Washington Avenue in 1840. During the mid-century it provided accommodation service along its main line south to Bell Road (now part of the city) and other intermediate stations on the way to Chester and, along what was termed the "Darby Improvement," offered service to many more villages in Delaware County. "At Darby, Moore's, Norwood, Sharon Hill, Ridley Park, and at other points," a writer for the railroad claimed in 1877, "a series of new places have sprung up, owing their existence entirely to the railroad and the facilities thereby afforded for reaching the countryside from the city streets." Every encouragement was given the city dweller to change his home base. The cost per mile of a single commutation ticket was approximately 2½¢ in the 1870s; on a monthly or annual basis, ½¢. Arrangements were made with real-estate agents to provide each new home owner with a complimentary railroad pass for each $1,000 spent on a house up to a limit of $10,000. If $2,500 were spent, for instance, the commuter would receive a pass good for two-and-one-half years. In addition, building materials for new homes were transported to the nearest station at one-half the usual freight rate. The railroad, of course, was one of the prime investors in real estate suitable for residential development. In the vicinity of Bonnaffon, now part of the city between Paschall and Bartram Park, the railroad owned several homes and a large tract of land suitable "for country seats," as an 1877 brochure put it. P.W. & B. executives played the real-estate speculation game all along the line.

If only the vision of bucolic suburban life entertained in the late 19th century could have been so perfectly realized. In the most economically privileged enclaves of suburban Philadelphia, large tracts of land could be held open, free from subdivision for many years. But these sanctuaries were increasingly difficult to maintain in the 1900s. Suburbia kept creeping farther away from the city—toward the end of the line at Paoli, southwest in the direction of West Chester through the classic country towns of Media, Darlington, and Westtown. Rarely did the prospective home owner turn to the New Jersey territory, just across the river and accessible by a complex network of railroads, including the West Jersey Seashore (controlled by the Pennsylvania) and the Reading's Atlantic City line. A merger of the South Jersey routes into the Pennsylvania-Reading Seashore Lines in 1932 put an effective end to the Reading's control of any part of the business.

From the mid-19th century on, the pleasant town of Haddonfield was only a little more than a half-hour away from Philadelphia; Woodbury was just as close. Haddonfield was first served by the Camden & Atlantic Railroad in 1854; Woodbury was reached from Camden in 1857 by the West Jersey Railroad. Both these lines were taken over by the Pennsylvania in 1871 as part of the lease of the United New Jersey Railroad and Canal Co. By 1883 Haddonfield residents were provided with excellent trains to Camden which connected there, via the Pennsylvania-controlled Camden & Philadelphia Steamboat Ferry, to Philadelphia. In 1896 the Pennsylvania started using the new Delair Bridge via North Philadelphia and Frankford Junction to serve Atlantic City travelers and residents of towns along that line, including Haddonfield. During the same year the Camden & Atlantic and West Jersey were merged with four other South Jersey lines to form the West Jersey Seashore Railroad. At this time the Reading was providing frequent suburban service to such Camden County communities as Audubon, Haddon Heights, Magnolia, and Clementon, all within an hour of Philadelphia via the South Street or Chestnut Street ferries and Camden.

Neither the Pennsylvania nor the Reading endeavored to assist the New Jersey suburban communities in their residential development to the extent done on the Pennsylvania side of the river. Prominent Philadelphia families had invested in South Jersey land for many years, but they much preferred the rolling hills of their own state to the relatively flat land across the river for residential purposes. In the early 1900s South Jersey was indeed the garden spot of the Garden State, a vast area of truck farming and small manufacturing enterprise. Although residents of Burlington, Camden, and Gloucester County towns had traveled to work in Philadelphia since the mid-19th century, their number was always small in proportion to the total number of commuters. The Delaware River served as a natural barrier between the two sides until well into the 20th century when the Walt Whitman Bridge connecting Camden and Philadelphia was opened in 1926.

In the 1930s Reading service along its main line to Atlantic City was reduced to a bare minimum. After 1932, the combined Pennsylvania-Reading Seashore Lines cut more and more of the service on all the branches. At the time there was no other choice as the territory covered was one of the most economically depressed in the East. After World War II, when there was demonstrable need for more trains, little

Ferry Terminal, Philadelphia & Reading Railroad (Atlantic Railroad), Chestnut Street, Philadelphia, 1900.

of the system was put back into effective operation. Ironically, it was this region which was finally attracting more and more Philadelphians in pursuit of moderately-priced homes and room for modest vegetable and flower gardens. Today residents of such densely populated areas as Cherry Hill and Moorestown depend on the automobile to get them to their city jobs. Driving became a way of life in the post-World War II period. Many of these new commuters probably never gave any thought to an alternative until the Lindenwold high-speed line was created from the remains of the Pennsylvania's old Atlantic City route in the 1960s. Work on this direct connection using the city's subway system and the Walt Whitman Bridge was first begun in 1952. Of all the high-speed lines established recently in the United States, it is the most successful.

Boston

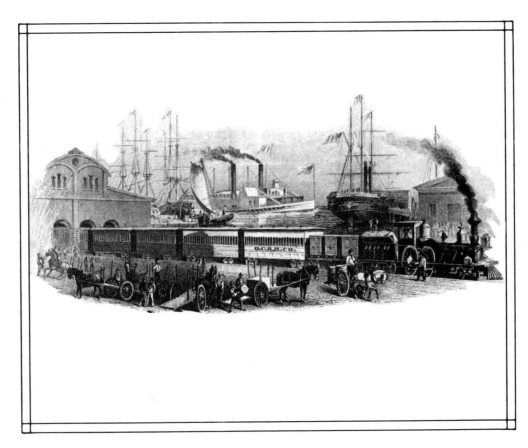

Vignette of Old Colony Railroad Station, Boston, from bank note, 1894.

One Great Suburb

If Boston is the Hub, the Railroads seen from the State House dome are the living spokes, which bind it to an outer circle of social and business relations. If these have carried off our men of enterprise in search of a larger market, they have brought back the wealth they accumulate, to beautify our estates and elevate our culture, and make of Massachusetts Bay, from Plymouth to Cape Anne, one great suburb in which the arts of cultivated life are brought to aid the native charms of country living.

—Robert S. Rantoul
Salem historian, 1871

Boston in the late 20th century is a quiet town for the railroads. An out-of-town visitor, probably arriving by plane, may never notice the two terminals which serve the city's remaining rail commuters. Both North and South Stations, removed from the modern activity of the business and tourist center, are rather forlorn outposts of a faded past—cheap plastic and plywood tacked down over once-handsome plaster ornamentation, lighting which makes reading difficult but emphasizes the emptiness of the waiting room, dirty and torn placards which serve as makeshift call boards. The stations certainly can't be called cheery, and they are most definitely not what any Bostonian could call proper. These are more than surface impressions: they are clear and present signs of a lingering illness. Death has been averted through the ministration of the Massachusetts Bay Transportation Authority, but the commuter lines are still on the critical list of problems that must be resolved if residents of the city's suburban areas are not to engulf the center of the Hub in a wave of automobile traffic and in a tangle of expressways.

One hopeful sign of progress is the revitalization of the former Boston & Albany's Newton Highlands branch as a rapid transit line running over ten miles from the city center to Riverside. This is an enterprise of the public MBTA, and further extension of Boston's transit system is planned for the future. In the meantime the authority is maintaining service to nearly eighty communities, some of which have been home to city businessmen since the 1840s. In 1848, it has been estimated, one-fifth of Boston's white collar managerial class lived in suburbia and used the train to reach work. In the years following the Civil War, this percentage was probably closer to one-fourth and may have risen as high as one-third. If Boston had not annexed the communities of Roxbury, West Roxbury, Charlestown, Brighton, and Dorchester in the 1860s and '70s, the city might have been left to only the very rich of Back Bay and the workers of the South End. Still left outside the city limits after annexation were Brookline and the vast town of Newton, as well as Cambridge and Somerville. These areas considered themselves not in the least urban, and fought off every attempt at annexation. New York City or Chicago politicians would have found ways to bring such recalcitrant enclaves under their control; in Boston the tradition of suburban living was too well developed by mid-century for the city to gather back a majority of its wayward children. As in St. Louis, this fragmentation, the encirclement of the urban core by suburbia, created severe economic problems, and their resolution on a regional basis had to await the boiling point in the mid-twentieth century.

If any institution is to blame for the suburban Boston diaspora, it was the railroad. As early as 1835 there were eight lines in existence, and three—the Boston & Worcester, the Boston & Providence, and the Boston & Lowell—began carrying passengers to country homes as early as 1845. There were even then people ready to move away from town. The reasons given at the time were of the usual sort: a more healthful climate, space for gardening and a safe place for children to play, a more "moral" environment free of taverns and other disreputable places and faces. By 1850 half the population was foreign-born, largely Irish, and this could not have pleased many of the natives who equated the Roman Church with the works of the devil. These evangelical Protestants, if of sufficient means, chose to be "born again," to start up a new order of life in the country no more than a few miles to a dozen from the city, but, nonethless, outside of it. Some of the families, of course, were so economically well-off as to afford both city and country residences, but the children stayed away from town a good part of the year. The railroads did everything they could to encourage this migration. Commutation rates between 1845 to the late '50s were set artificially low. By the time it was discovered that the fares—some averaging as low as 1½¢ a mile—were a drain on the financial resources of the railroad companies and had to be raised, suburban businessmen were sufficiently well entrenched to fight off any attempts to exact very much more for service. The rates crept up slowly over the years, but at no time did they begin to cover the actual costs of operation. The railroads, obviously, made their profits from shipping freight. The gentlemen who ran Boston's commuter lines, many of them suburban residents, never did push their case for higher commuter rates very hard. As late as 1925, the assistant to the president of the Boston & Maine admitted, "The concessions . . . by New England railroads are more liberal as to conditions than any form of multiple-ride transportation sold to suburban riders in New York, Philadelphia, or Baltimore." How could the railroads justify such largesse?

> It is essential to the physical health and the quality of citizenship, of urban populations especially, that families be raised away from the congested centers of population. To do so, low rates for daily travel by rail between home and business are a requisite.

The demographic pattern of suburban settlement in the Boston area followed that established elsewhere—from inner to outer circles. By 1848, according to historian Charles J. Kennedy, there were eighty-three commuter stations within fifteen miles of Boston. Many of the neighborhoods were also within range of street railway service, a development which was underway by the late '50s. The spread of an economical transit system, first in the form of horse-drawn cars, opened up these outlying districts to the middle class who had found that the steam railroads' fares, however equitable in theory, were in fact too much to deduct from their weekly paychecks. As was inevitable, however, many of the gentlemen who could afford such an expense started to move yet farther west, south, and north from the city in search of the country life. So it would go for many, many years—one economic group leaving behind room for the one below it until all the commutable metropolitan territory had been explored and settled. In the mid-1900s, a return to the historic center-city core, the starting point of the long migration, was underway, but there was no significant shrinkage of the suburban crescent. During this same period the semi-circular research and manufacturing belt around Boston formed by Route 128 defined the future for a vast majority of people. Boston had indeed become at last, in the minds of most suburban residents, a city for only the wealthy and the poor.

The Boston & Albany Railroad

Trains today to the western suburbs over the tracks of the former Boston & Albany take riders as far as Riverside on one line and Framingham on another. Considering the vicissitudes of the railroad, controlled from 1900 until recent years by the New York Central, it is nothing less than miraculous that there are trains to board and tracks to follow. Riders on the rapid transit line to Riverside through Brookline and Newton, a route which assumed its present form in 1959, are following a path first carved out to Brookline in 1847, and later extended as part of the Highland Branch of the Boston & Albany. The Framingham line from South Station follows the Boston & Albany's former main line, stopping at Newtonville, West Newton, Auburndale, three places in the Wellesley area, and Natick. It is this route which was first established in 1834 by the railroad's predecessor, the Boston & Worcester,

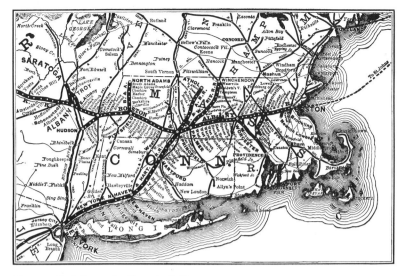

Boston & Albany Railroad, 1893.

as far west as Newton. Such inner-city stops as Cottage Farm (later renamed University), Allston, and Brighton—now skipped by the railroad—formed the centers of Boston's first suburban neighborhoods.

According to historian Charles J. Kennedy, requests for special commuter fares on the Boston & Worcester were first made in 1835, within a year of commencing service. A second-class passenger car was added to a regular train and it could be ridden for a cost twenty percent to fifty percent below that of first class. This accommodation, however, was only a temporary and insufficient response to a growing need. By 1845 relatively inexpensive rates had been set to encourage commutation, and during the same period the Boston & Worcester began regular suburban passenger service as far as West Newton. By the time the Boston & Worcester and the Western Railroad of Massachusetts were merged to form the Boston & Albany in 1866, the commuting territory was well defined and extended some twenty miles west of the city. The Highland branch was linked to the main line at Riverside and riders could choose to travel into the city one of two ways—through Newton and Brookline or via the main line—on what became known as the Circuit Line. In the play *The Colored Man Who Cries the Trains*, William Dean Howells recreated the melodious chant of the train announcer calling out the stops:

> Cars ready for College Farms . . . Longwood . . . Chestnut Hill . . . Brookline . . . Newton Centre . . . Newton Highlands . . . Waban . . . Riverside . . . and all stations between Riverside and Boston . . . . Circuit Line train now ready on track number three.

In 1850 Brighton was considered the first regular suburban stop on the main line and was described in a contemporary travel guide as "the residence of many people of wealth, who have . . . erected costly residences." There was a hint of things to come, however, in the admission that "The extensive and numerous butchering establishments . . . which are scattered over the town, are a serious objection to the choice of Brighton, as a place of residence unconnected with business." It was suggested that one could continue on to Newton Corner or West Newton, both of which are "pleasantly situated," and "becoming deservedly popular." And, of course, there was Brookline, an eminently respectable community which could be reached at the time via the one-and-one-half-mile-long Brookline Branch Railroad, a subsidiary of the Boston & Worcester. Longwood, one of the first stops in Brookline, was a particularly bucolic area of gently rolling hills and handsome

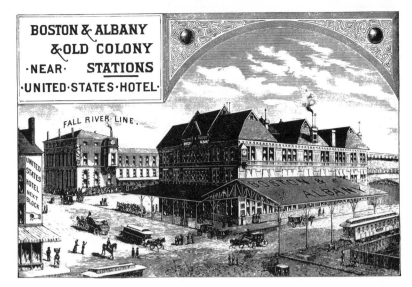

Boston & Albany and Old Colony Stations, Kneeland Street, Boston, 1880s.

Longwood Station, Brookline, Massachusetts, Boston & Albany Railroad, c. 1933.

Newton Highlands Station, Newton, Massachusetts, Boston & Albany Railroad, 1950s.

residences. Longwood had been laid out by David Sears, a Boston entrepreneur, according to a definite plan which included as architectural centerpieces a handsome railroad station and a Gothic parish building, Christ Church (Sears Chapel).

The determination of Longwood and other Brookline residents to keep their community a pleasant and peaceful one was challenged through the second half of the 19th century. An electrified street railway to Boston was opened up along Beacon Street in 1899 by the Metropolitan Railroad Co., and the inevitable result was increasing urbanization. Later, a Brookline historian, John Gould Curtis, reported: "electric trams . . . represented a necessary concession to public convenience." They were preferable to what had been proposed ten years earlier—an elevated railroad. This, Curtis asserted, "was a dreadful thing, to be opposed with all vigor. New York's elevated steam railways were certainly not a reassuring example." Sections of Brookline lying along the path of the old railroad, however, had been so well planned and guarded that they were not inundated by real-estate development. Such new building as did occur was studiously designed to blend in with the already existing townscape. The Longwood Towers apartment complex and a host of other Tudor Gothic multiple dwelling units of the early 1900s were carefully sited and shaped to complement the community of one-family homes.

Chestnut Hill Station, Newton, Massachusetts, Boston & Albany Railroad, 1908.

For those who felt that Brookline and Newton were slipping too close to the city for comfort, there was always the Wellesley, Natick, and Framingham area farther west to be explored. As early as the 1870s, Wellesley Hills was described as the "seat of many elegant residences of citizens doing business in Boston." In 1875 Wellesley College was established by Boston lawyer Henry Fowle Durant and given a campus of more than 300 acres. Many of America's late 19th-century women's colleges were planted in the green fields of suburbia—Bryn Mawr, Beaver, and Sarah Lawrence, among them—and provided a cultural tone very much in keeping with that desired by upper-class residents. The natural beauty of the Wellesley landscape and the civilizing influence of the college drew many wealthy families to settle there. By 1893 there were sixteen daily trains in each direction serving Wellesley Farms, Wellesley Hills, Wellesley, and Natick. All the main-line suburban trains began and ended their runs at what was then South Framingham station, a handsome terminal designed by Henry Hobson Richardson. The original center of this classic country town—made up of three villages first settled in 1640—was the stop designated as Framingham. Because of the railroad's importance, the center of commercial life shifted to the south.

Top, *Wellesley (Massachusetts) Station, 1959;* above, *South Framingham (Massachusetts) Station, 1890s. Both, Boston & Albany Railroad.*

The New York, New Haven & Hartford Railroad

Boston's south and southwestern commuting territory came under the control of the New Haven Railroad in the 1890s when the Old Colony and the New York & New England lines were leased. Along with the Old Colony came the Providence division, formerly the Boston & Providence, one of the most important of Boston's early commuter railroads. It has been said that the New Haven "did for the Northeast what Boston and other money did for the West—rebuilt and remodeled inadequate lines, consolidated competing or parallel roads, reorganized and re-equipped the various parts, spending money as it never had been spent before." This was written in 1929, and the spending part is certainly true. There is also truth

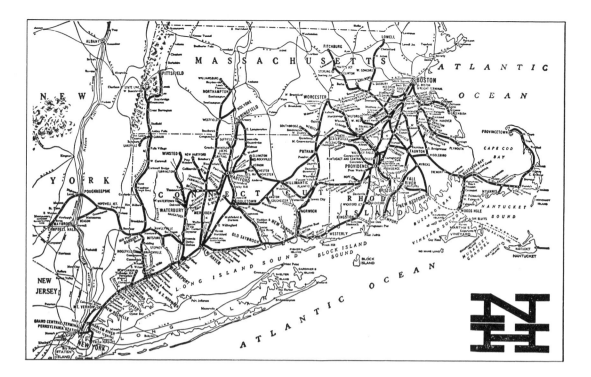

New York, New Haven & Hartford Railroad, 1957.

to the statement that the rabbit warren of branch lines was brought under more rational control by the New Haven. It is debatable, however, whether the Boston metropolitan area profited greatly from the helping hand of an absentee landlord. If direction of the company during the early decades of the 1900s had been less shaky, much good might have resulted. Instead, many of Boston's suburbs to the south gradually lost direct service to the city.

Through acquisition of the Massachusetts and Rhode Island lines, the New Haven had captured a lucrative intercity passenger and freight market. Only the Boston & Albany, controlled by the New York Central after 1900, posed any possible threat to the hegemony of the New Haven in the area to the south and west of Boston, and the New York Central wasn't about to upset its private understanding with the New Haven. The two companies had cooperated in entirely removing their only serious southern New England rival, the New York & New England, from the map in the 1890s. The Old Colony with its Plymouth, Taunton, Cape Cod, and Providence divisions provided the New Haven with entry into hundreds of commuting villages and manufacturing towns in the southeast corner of the state as well as in Rhode Island and eastern Connecticut.

Only two of the Old Colony's lines survive today, and both were established, at least in part, by the Boston & Providence before it was merged with the former company. Trains are routed to the southwest from South Station and, on one line, follow the Boston & Providence main line stopping at Canton Junction, Canton, Stoughton, Sharon, and Mansfield. Beyond this point, the economic and geographic orientation of the riders is toward Providence. Service on this route is supplemented with stops at Mount Hope, Hyde Park, and Readville. These three villages are located within Boston proper, but existed independently until the late 1800s.

The second former Old Colony and Boston & Providence line serves the inner-city neighborhoods of Forest Hills, Roslindale, Bellevue, and West Roxbury; it then

Above left, *Dedham (Massachusetts) Station, Boston & Providence Railroad, 1880s;* at right, *Charles River Valley line, including the West Roxbury Extension, New York, New Haven & Hartford Railroad, 1907.*

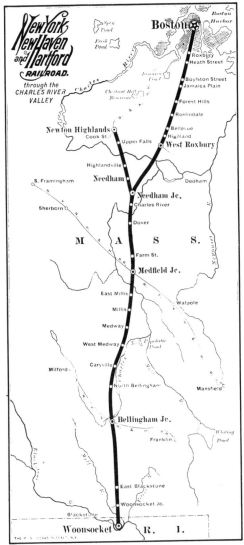

proceeds to Needham Junction where it joins the former tracks of the New York & New England's Central division. In 1907 the New Haven created this link between the two railroads and termed it the "New West Roxbury Extension." It made commuting to the Needham area considerably easier. Prior to this time, many Needham commuters traveled out to Cook Street in Newton Highlands on the Boston & Albany and then had their cars attached to a New York & New England engine that pulled them south two miles to Needham Heights (then called Highlandville) or three miles to Needham center. With the new extension, Needham became especially attractive to prospective commuters; it was served by twenty-five trains each way on a workday basis. Its location, according to the New Haven's publicity agents, was "particularly picturesque and healthful, the latter condition being no doubt largely due to the extensive growths of pine trees." But there were people there, too—4,500 of them in 1907. Fifty years later, there were at least 25,000.

Needham was not, however, the end of the line. Commuters who wished to travel farther south into the Charles River valley could do so — at that time — from Needham Junction. Rents and building-lot prices were considerably lower in such small manufacturing towns as Medfield and Medway than they were in the Needham area. "Nature has been lavish in her endowment of this locality," the New Haven wrote in 1907, "characterized by high and rolling hills, woodland and meadow, sloping gently to the valley of the Charles River, which winds, delightfully, now to the right, then to the left, affording scenery and situations in the highest degree attractive and inviting." Homes in the Medfield area, for instance, could be rented for about $15 a month; building lots were priced at an average of $100. Service on this southern end of the former New York & New England line was cut drastically in the 1930s; by the '50s there was only one train each way, and now there are none.

The only other remaining commuter line serving the southern suburban territory is one that was inherited by the New Haven from the New York & New England. It had served as the latter's main line through the city en route to Woonsocket, Rhode Island, and on via Willimantic, Hartford, and Waterbury, Connecticut, to the line's terminus at Fishkill-on-Hudson, New York. The New York & New England provided convenient service to such inner-city neighborhoods as Dorchester, Mattapan, Hyde Park, and Readville. Now this line begins its stops at Endicott and then continues on to Islington, Norwood, Windsor Gardens, Plimptonville, Walpole, and Norfolk to terminate at Franklin. The "Norfolk County Express" still runs to Boston each morning from Franklin at 7:20, but this is only one of the eight scheduled runs each day in both directions.

Service on these surviving southern routes (as well as the western Framingham line inherited from the Boston & Albany) is operated by the Boston & Maine, the last remaining local rail transportation corporation, under contract with the Massachusetts Bay Transportation Authority. The symbol which appears on all the MBTA schedules is the figure of the Revolutionary War "Minute Man" and has been used by the Boston & Maine since the mid-1940s. Hopefully, he will be able to guard against further violation of the once-proud trains which served some of Boston's oldest suburbs long before such western and northern outposts as Wayland, Weston, Pride's Crossing, and Hamilton were anything more than exurban retreats for the wealthy.

Before the New Haven arrived on the scene, the Old Colony Railroad had been an important part of the suburban landscape. Many of the towns it served were rather

New York & New England Railroad, 1893.

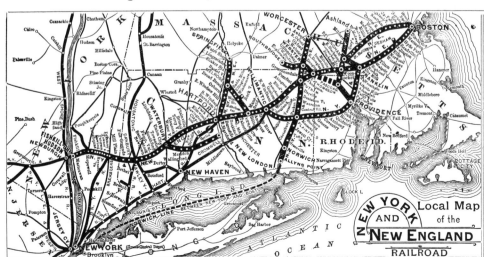

Above, *Sagamore (Massachusetts) Station, Old Colony Railroad, 1890s;* middle, *Middleboro (Massachusetts) Station, Old Colony Railroad, 1890s;* below left, *North Easton (Massachusetts) Station, Old Colony Railroad, 1890s;* below right, *Boston & Providence Station, Park Square, Boston, 1889.*

smart places in which to live during the 19th century, and the railroad itself was a spiffy affair. Opened in 1845, the Old Colony ran to the then-fashionable South Shore and the equally attractive Dorchester and Ashmont neighborhoods which became part of the city in the 1870s. The Dorchester & Milton Railroad had been leased in 1848. "Old Colony cars," a company historian recalled, "were painted yellow, and when fresh from the shop with 'Old Colony' in fancy letters on the side, and decorations each side of the name and on the end of each car, nothing could compare with them for beauty." The original main line proceeded south from a station on Kneeland Street and passed through South Boston, Crescent Avenue, Savin Hill, Harrison Square, and Neponset, terminating some eleven miles later in South Braintree. The Shawmut branch left the main line at Harrison Square for Milton and Mattapan; a second branch, the Granite, served East Milton and West Quincy from Atlantic station on the main line. "These sections," a railroad spokesman enthused in 1889, "form a thickly settled region, the towns and villages having beautiful situations after the heart of the city is left behind, the Neponset valley, the Blue Hills of Milton, the heights about Quincy . . . presenting scenery unequalled elsewhere in New England."

The famous Fall River Railroad, an early enterprise of the Borden family of that city, became a part of the Old Colony system in 1854. The most illustrious of the trains was that which carried passengers to and from the New York-Fall River steamboat line. Service began on a cooperative basis between the two railroads in 1847, and was continued until the late 1930s. On a more prosaic level, however, there were several villages along the Fall River route of great interest to Bostonians. North Easton, the country home of Oliver and Oakes Ames, Boston financiers and builders of the Union Pacific, is one of the most remarkable — even today. Here, with the patronage of Frederick L. Ames, the son of Oliver, Henry Hobson Richardson built some of his most successful buildings in the mid-1880s, including the Old Colony station. This structure, perhaps more than any other, illustrates architectural critic Vincent Scully's statement that the Richardson stations "were both urban and suburban place-fixing masses adjusted to expanding suburban patterns along the commuting railroad lines." Provincial towns such as North Easton, coming into their own as outposts of urban life, required definition of a sophisticated sort. Richardson's monumental but naturally graceful style stamped the village as one of importance and social distinction. Although North Easton would continue to be best known throughout the world for its production of shovels made at the Ames works, it had been "improved" in a way that pleased the men who worked in Boston and their visitors to the country.

The Boston & Providence, the oldest of the Old Colony's divisions, was leased in 1888, and with it came perhaps Boston's most beautiful terminal. Located where Back Bay station now stands, the Park Square building was designed by the firm of Peabody and Stearns and was opened in the 1870s. Edwin Bacon's *Dictionary of Boston* (1886) contains a careful contemporary description of the building:

> A great marble hall in the centre of the spacious head house, imposing in its general effect and magnificent in its architectural beauty, was the strikingly effective feature of the interior. From this hall opened the large and well-appointed waiting rooms, dining-rooms, baggage-rooms, and so forth; while from a fine gallery surrounding it at a height of twenty-one feet, access was given to a travelers' reading-room, a billiard-room, and to the offices of the company. The long train house, with monitor roof, opened from the farther end of the central hall, approaching by a dignified flight of steps the width of the building, it being below the level of the head house. The façade of the handsome exterior facing Columbus Avenue close beside Park Square, was marked by a lofty and fine proportioned tower, high up in which was a tower-clock illuminated at night.

It was not long before the Old Colony moved many of its trains and executives from Kneeland Street to Park Square. Until the building of South Station, on the site of the New York & New England station, in 1899, suburbanites bound for the inner-city suburbs of Jamaica Plain and Mount Hope and for the village of Hyde Park (to be annexed in 1912) shared the facilities with intercity travelers to Providence and

South Station, Boston, 1898.

further east. In addition, the Park Square terminal was used by commuters from the Roslindale, Highland, West Roxbury, and Dedham stops of the Boston & Providence. The stations along the main Providence division and its branch lines were extremely attractive stone or masonry structures which greatly enhanced the suburban neighborhoods. Park Square, however, was an exceptional landmark, and even monumental South Station, shared with the Boston & Albany, could not begin to compare in beauty.

The history of the New York & New England Railroad lines (previous to 1873, the New York, Hartford & Erie) which connect Boston and Franklin and form part of the Needham route is so complex that its retelling would require the work of several cartographers and economic historians. Briefly, the railroad was an amalgam of twelve short lines which crossed central New England. It is by no means certain that the nefarious operators of this combine, most often on the verge of bankruptcy, had any serious interest in serving Boston's commuters. Their ultimate aim was to siphon freight and intercity passenger traffic bound for the New York area away from the expanding New Haven and New York Central combine. Back of the New York & New England were much larger interests such as the Reading and Erie that were unable to reach any farther east than the Hudson. By 1893, the railroad was hopelessly bankrupt, as was its then parent company, the Reading. Control was easily grasped by the New Haven in 1895 and the road was renamed the New England Railroad.

The Boston & Maine Railroad

Boston's last surviving rail corporation has been kept alive by the Massachusetts Bay Transportation Authority. Death has been prematurely declared several times over the past 130 years, most recently when the executives who did so much to ruin the New Haven Railroad in the 1950s moved on to the Boston & Maine. Compared with the Boston & Albany, the Old Colony, the Boston & Lowell, and the Boston & Providence, the Boston & Maine was one of the latecomers on the suburban scene. Commuters were carried to Medford and other nearby towns to the northwest as early as the 1840s when the railroad was granted permission to extend its tracks to the city from Wilmington, but the bulk of the suburban territory which exists today did not belong to or was not developed by the Boston & Maine until the 1880s or '90s. The reasons for the lag are twofold. Most city families seeking year-round country homes did not settle to the north of the city until later in the century. Bacon's *Dictionary of Boston* defined the principal suburban territory as it had then developed:

> The most famous and fashionable of all the suburbs lie to the southward and westward, with the beautiful rural estates of Boston's merchant princes. Milton, Brookline and Newton, in particular, stand in the front rank in this respect, although but little in advance of Dorchester and West Roxbury.

This is not to say that development was not occurring elsewhere in earlier years. "The northern suburbs also contain many delightful estates . . . ," Bacon reported. A great number of these homes, especially on the North Shore, however, were built only as seasonal retreats, as summer places, and the railroads could not count on year-round commuter patrons. The regular riders in many of the coastal areas were few in number compared to the summer people. The Boston & Maine faced stiff competition from both the Boston & Lowell and the Eastern Railroad for the remaining passengers. Until the merger of the three lines in the 1880s, the railroads scrapped among themselves for suburban business. Although the competition was healthy in many respects and was certainly in the best American tradition of free enterprise, it was highly inefficient and costly. Symbolic of the new united way of the Boston & Maine of the 1890s was the first North Station, an amalgam of buildings pulled together in 1894 and first called Union Station. It served both the new Boston & Maine system and the Fitchburg Railroad. In 1900 the Fitchburg also came under control of the larger system.

Malden, Medford, Somerville, Watertown, Waltham, Cambridge—all these towns to the north and northwest of Boston grew into cities during the slow rise to power of the Boston & Maine from the 1840s to the '90s. Those closest to the city, in particular Somerville and Cambridge on the Fitchburg line, developed first as commuter-railroad territory and then became "streetcar" suburbs with the arrival of rapid transit. The Fitchburg, for instance, ran a special branch to Harvard College in the late '40s, but the line was discontinued in 1856 when it was proved to be unprofitable. The streetcar companies could serve nearby suburban areas quite inexpensively, but could not extend their lines into the country. Because of its unique position as a college town, a large part of Cambridge retained a pleasant, upper-class suburban air well into the 20th century. This was not true, however, of some other adjoining towns which made room for the expansion of industry which was not welcome in Brookline, Newton, or Dorchester. A professional writer traveling the Boston & Maine's main line in 1887 recorded the passing suburban scene as he saw it:

> Somerville does not show to good advantage from the cars nor does Chelsea; but when we get past, and out upon the meadows of the Mystic and can look backward to the left at the hills of West Somerville and Medford (the latter crowned by the

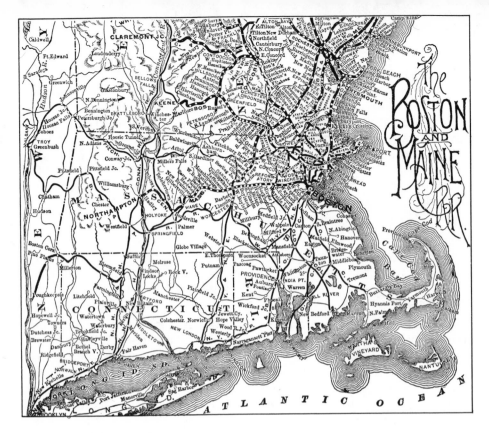

Boston & Maine Railroad, 1893.

clustered buildings of Tuft's College), we begin to enjoy the real country. . . . The town contains the homes of many prominent business men of Boston.

Similar words of praise were saved for Malden and Melrose.

By the time the Fitchburg was merged with the Boston & Maine in 1900, the suburban flight had gained momentum and distance. Such historic towns as Concord, Winchester, Woburn, Salem, and Beverly were drawn within the commuting perimeters. In the 1920s other more rural areas—Wayland and Weston almost due west; Lincoln and Acton to the northwest; Hamilton and Wenham to the north; Pride's Crossing and Manchester to the northeast—were viewed with serious interest as providing the real "charm" of country life. The Essex County communities between Beverly and Rockport on the Gloucester branch of the Eastern Railroad had been favorite summer colonies since the Civil War. "The coast was captured by city Yankees," according to a North Shore historian, "following the trail cindered . . . by the Gloucester branch" in 1847. For many years, however, Pride's Crossing station, a typical stop, consisted of nothing but a shelter and a flagman, in this case a member of the Pride family of farmers, "stone deaf and so indifferent to the approach of the train that the passengers had to do their own flagging." By the 1890s something more was needed. A station was built and the stop was listed in the regular schedules for the first time. The "Flying Fisherman," a reserved express train, sped between Boston and Rockport each day during the succeeding sixty years and provided special comfort for the affluent commuter. Even today there is one morning express which brings the Pride's Crossing resident into Boston in forty minutes. A similar train leaves North Station at 4:56 p.m., a comfortable banker's hour.

146

Melrose and the Middlesex Fells region, closer to the city, became a favorite retreat for city businessmen during the same period and developed more rapidly as a year-round community. Located on the Boston & Maine's main line, it had been largely overlooked until the 1880s because of its rocky terrain that impressed neither farmers nor get-rich-quick land developers. This difficult landscape, however, was, in the words of a Boston & Maine commentator, "a great boon to the city men":

> Among its broken hills, crags, and prairie nooks, beside its dancing streams, and under the shade of its oaks and chestnuts, have now been built scores of beautiful country homes, picturesque in outward appearance, and luxurious within. . . .

Today, schedules on what is termed the "North Side" line of the Boston & Maine, terminating at Reading, reflect the importance of the suburban Melrose area. There is a special morning and an evening express, stopping at Melrose Cedar Park and Melrose Highlands, and several other rush-hour trains which make the trip back and forth to the city an easy one.

To the northwest of the city the communities of Kendall Green and Weston, Lincoln, and Concord on what was the Fitchburg's main line prospered in the early

Waltham (Massachusetts) Depot, Boston & Maine, 1898.

1900s as Somerville and Waltham declined in the esteem of those seeking either a quiet country scene or a respectable address or both. Lincoln, which became the home of architect Walter Gropius in the late 1930s, emerged as one of the wealthiest communities in the Boston area and as a favorite spot for the building of contemporary homes by professional men from Cambridge and Boston. Lincoln today is the first stop on the evening 5:05 "Paul Revere Express" and is served by two express trains each morning.

Probably the most extensive suburban service originating from the north side of Boston in the late 1800s was that provided by the Boston & Lowell, after 1887 part of the Boston & Maine. Almost a century later, the line to Lowell has more scheduled passenger trains than any other. The difference now is that rather than twenty-three stations, as in the 1890s, there are nine. All of the stops in Cambridge and

Top left, *Weston (Massachusetts) Station, 1959;* bottom left, *Hamilton & Wenham (Massachusetts) Station, 1950s;* top right, *Lincoln (Massachusetts) Station, 1930s;* bottom right, *Winchester (Massachusetts) Station, 1960s. All, Boston & Maine Railroad.*

Somerville have been eliminated, leaving Tufts (College Hill as it was called earlier) as the first station for modern-day commuters. Few of the trains, however, stop here or at the next station, West Medford, but are headed for Woburn with intermediate stops at Wedgemere, Winchester Centre, and Cross Street; or for Lowell with stops at Wilmington and North Billerica. This latter section of the line farthest from Boston is particularly well equipped with express trains—three in the evening and one in the morning.

Suburban service today on the Boston & Maine is designed primarily to suit the needs of the commuter who lives some distance from the city. A New Yorker or Chicagoan would hardly find the distance between North Station and Woburn—ten miles—or from the same point and Lincoln—seventeen miles—much of a trip. Boston, however, is the smallest of the major American rail-commuting cities. The steam railroads which started so early in Boston, which should have made the city one of the great American rail centers, retreated from neighborhoods adjacent to the city in the advance of the streetcar system. This was particularly true in the contiguous areas west and north. The reasons for the abandonment of service to what were to become urban areas are to a large degree financial. The backers of the steam-railroad lines could not begin to match the fare schedule of the streetcar lines. When four of the largest of these joined together as the West End Company and electrified the system, there really was little left for the steam railroads to do on the northern and western edges of the city. The men who had invested in the early steam lines became interested in Western ventures—in Chicago, Omaha, San Francisco—and found a more secure resting place for their money. Back home these same people who ultimately decided when trains should run and where they should stop were quite content to maintain suburban service to the outer reaches of the territory. Except for the Boston & Albany's Highland branch and some service on the former Boston & Providence's main line through Dorchester and adjoining neighborhoods, the city and its urban satellites were for all intents and purposes abandoned.

The Boston & Maine's urban presence was most strikingly emphasized in the 1890s when the original North (or Union Station) complex was opened. For the first time in the century, all the trains serving the northwestern and northern suburbs were coordinated behind the façade of one operating rail corporation. Architecturally, however, the structure was an artificial construct. As one Boston commentator, Edwin Bacon, said at the time: "North Station was a patchwork affair—clever patchwork, however, in which were utilized the old Eastern station at one end and the Lowell station at the other, with a brave exterior show of ornamented stone columns between." It was, indeed, a clever show. The building lasted only until 1927 when it was replaced by the present North Station/Boston Garden affair. The railroad—sustained in its worst trials by a loyal band of commuters who could not tolerate any other form of travel—somehow survived the sham.

Union Station (North Station), Boston, Boston & Maine Railroad and the Fitchburg Railroad, 1890s.

Chicago

Illinois Central Station at South Water Street and railroad yards, Chicago, 1865.

Railroading and Real Estate

I am planning to subdivide the tract and start a town of my own. If your railroad will cooperate with me in this development, you and I can do business.

The speaker was Paul Cornell, a Chicago land speculator and watch manufacturer, and the time the early 1850s. The proposition was being made to the Illinois Central Railroad, then in the process of building its main line south from Chicago to Kankakee, Illinois. Cornell would sell the railroad a sixty-acre tract from 300 acres that he owned south of the city *if* the company would provide service to an area to be called Hyde Park. "My price for the sixty," Cornell informed management, "will be $30 an acre, and if your railroad will work with me in building up a residential community every acre will double or treble in value in ten years' time." He was right. Within five years of the establishment of the "Hyde Park Express" and a station at 53rd Street in 1856, the land was worth at least three times the original price. In 1856 there was only a handful of pioneers living in the south-side territory; by 1860 there were several hundred, and stations at Oakland, Kenwood, and Woodlawn had been added to that of 53rd Street.

Thus was established the first formal suburban train service west of Philadelphia. The same pattern of land development was to be repeated in succeeding years by combines representing the interests of the railroads and real-estate speculators. Chicago was not without its well-established villages which *became* suburbs over time—Evanston, Geneva, Downer's Grove, Wheaton were among them—but, unlike the older Eastern metropolitan areas, the northeastern Illinois countryside was much less defined and therefore much more open to planned development. Sinclair Lewis wrote in *Main Street* (1920) of a small Midwestern town far removed from any city, but the situation he described so well in that novel was very much like that known in the second half of the the 19th century to the north, west, and south of Chicago.

> The East remembered generations when there had been no railroad, and had no awe of it; but here the railroads had been before time was. The towns had been staked out on barren prairie as convenient points for future train-halts; and back in 1860 and 1870 there had been much profit, much opportunity to found aristocratic families, in the possession of advance knowledge as to where the towns would arise.

The development of the city of Chicago and many of its towns progressed in lock-step with that of the railroads. The managers, in consort with their bankers, charted out not only the course of future settlement in the West, but shaped the suburban neighborhoods that would be home for workers as well as businessmen. Prophetic powers were hardly needed to succeed; only sufficient funds were required to participate in the speculation. During the late 1800s, the basic system of suburban service emerged in a form that has practically defied significant change to the present day. The Chicago & North Western, the Burlington, the Illinois Central, and the Rock Island companies firmly established their rights to certain sections of the metropolitan area from the 1850s to the '70s, and stayed with them; the Milwaukee Road was a latecomer to the scene in the '80s. Unlike the situation in Boston, Philadelphia, or New York, a great maze of crisscrossing, competitive lines was not to develop beyond the city, and not until the early 1900s, with electrification and the rise of the interurbans, did residents of suburbia have any choice at all in the means of commutation. The interurban boom, of course, proved to be a bust and only one of the three major companies, the South Shore, remains alive to tell the story. The old steam railroads were so carefully laid out that they wouldn't die—even during the years following World War II.

Much of the early suburban territory closest to the city was annexed from the 1850s until the early 1900s. Hyde Park and its south-side neighbors—Englewood, Kensington, Calumet, and South Chicago—had been made a part of the city by 1900. Austin on the west side, and Irving Park, Rogers Park, Ravenswood, and Lake View to the north were annexed during the same period. Most of these neighborhoods had been laid out by land improvement companies in the 1860s and '70s with the cooperation of the railroads. Both to the north and west there was service on the North Western with as many as fourteen trains daily in 1874. Growth in the city was so rapid following the Civil War, however, that even villages that would always remain outside the city limits developed very rapidly. Evanston, called in 1874 "important, intellectually ambitious, wealthy Evanston," led the way on the North Shore in growth of population. By this time, however, nearly all the villages which would later constitute a golden chain of suburban affluence had been "laid out" for development and were sited along the North Western's Milwaukee route which followed the Lake Michigan shore. Much the same story can be told of such western villages as Oak Park and Lombard on the Galena line of the North Western, and Riverside and Hinsdale on the Burlington main line. To the southwest, the Rock Island Railroad participated in the development of the Beverly Hills and Morgan Park neighborhoods and of Blue Island.

From 1860 to 1871, the year of the Great Fire, Chicago's population more than tripled to 325,000. Two years later it was estimated at having grown by another 100,000. The fire stopped few from coming to what was the Houston of the day, and increasing numbers of the settlers were foreign born. If the natives had not been frightened away from the city by the catastrophe, many did feel ill-at-ease in a city which was becoming crowded by people with whom they had little that they wanted to share. Chicago kept growing with the influx of cheap immigrant labor, and the Protestant establishment of the time began to retreat to the hinterlands of Lake Forest and Hinsdale or closer to Evanston and Oak Park. The railroads were in place to serve the "displaced," and since the late 1860s had provided special fares for commutation to encourage the outward flow. Ironically, fares throughout the country were roughly the same for special immigrant trains westward or for the now-ubiquitous commuter passenger trains. Railroad company officials and board members, almost all of whom dabbled in real estate, were eager, of course, to make good on their suburban land investments. By the 1890s villages of a thousand residents were on their way to becoming small cities, and some became incorporated as such. Many were "dry" towns, determined to fight the threat of rum. Almost all had at least Congregational or Presbyterian, Methodist, and Episcopal churches, and little mention is made in the literature of the day of the Roman. Membership in the Democratic party, that seat of rebellion, was best kept hidden.

In 19th-century discussions of the values of suburban life, the emphasis was always on matters of health, comfort, and recreation, rather than on concerns of religion, race, or ethnic origin. The passenger departments of the railroads did their best to make life seem attractive to prospective home owners. It was not that difficult. An 1895 pamphlet, "Chicago Suburbs on the Chicago, Burlington & Quincy R.R.," presented a convincing argument: "Out of reach of the smoke and grime and dust, and yet completely in touch with the city, are hundreds and hundreds of beautiful homes . . . . Nearly all of the suburban districts in which these homes are located are, in point of time, nearer to the business part of the city than Lake View, Hyde Park, Englewood . . . . Trains that run to and from them during the day and night carry their residents to and from business much more pleasantly, much more quickly, and almost always more promptly on time than residents within the city are carried one-fifth the distance on the streetcars." In case the point of suburban convenience and ease was not sufficiently understood, the vicissitudes of inner-city travel were horrifically recounted:

> In order to travel over a distance less than 4 miles from the City Hall the hapless traveler on the streetcars has for the same or greater length of time to cling like a fly to steps or straps or platform guard. He is jostled, crushed, choked with dust or bedraggled with rain and mud.

In truth, because of reasonable commutation rates (rarely amounting to more than 2¢ a mile) and special rush-hour express service, the trip back and forth between country and city was not all that difficult for a majority of the middle and upper-middle classes of the late 19th century. Those with the highest incomes could afford to travel the farthest, and did. In the early 1900s Colonel Robert R. McCormick could enjoy his Wheaton farm, the Dunhams their castle in Wayne, the Insulls a home on the Fox River at Geneva—and still maintain their economic and cultural ties to the city. As early as 1874 it was written that "The old fogeyish idea that a residence in a suburb or in the country must perforce be unprovided with all the comforts of a city home, has long since exploded." Not until railroad service began to fall apart in the 1940s did this pastoral image of the good life begin to fall into disrepute.

The Illinois Central Railroad

Of all Chicago's commuter railroads, the Illinois Central has remained the most efficiently-run over the years. Because of the development of the city, the principal territory that the railroad has served since the end of the 19th century until World War II has been intraurban. Chicago, however enlarged, has remained a city of distinct neighborhoods. Even the expressways of the 1950s and '60s did not obliterate the majority of ethnic and cultural "towns" which arose in preceding decades. The central portion of Hyde Park has survived as the focus of the University of Chicago's main campus activities, and nearby Kenwood, once described as "the Lake Forest of the South," has also benefitted from association with the university. To the southwest, on the Illinois Central's Blue Island branch from Kensington, residential development assumed a low profile, one maintained well into the mid-1900s. Other areas on the south side—South Shore on the South Chicago branch and various communities along the main line—have retained a pleasant, residential atmosphere for many years and have helped to keep the Illinois Central very much in the suburban railroading business.

Gradually during the 1880s and '90s industry made its way to the perimeters of these enclaves. George Pullman established his model manufacturing town near Lake Calumet in the early '80s, and by 1893 there were 12,000 residents. In the meantime, South Chicago had developed as an important center of steel production. To the south of these two sections lay a vast area of country villages—Riverdale, Harvey, Homewood, Flossmoor—which early in the 1900s absorbed more and more of the overflow of workers and businessmen from the city. Suburban service was gradually extended into the new territory, finally reaching as far as Richton. Ridership climbed, too, on the branches and the main line. Unlike most other Chicago commuter lines, ridership did not peak in 1929 but continued to grow until after World War II. Electrification of the entire suburban system in 1926 helped the railroad to meet the challenges of the Depression years, but there were other factors in the successful operation: despite some competition from public transit, the Illinois Central's management continued to provide good service to communities which had been absorbed by the city in the 1880s and '90s, and to price it reasonably; trains brought businessmen directly into the central business district along the lake rather than to the outer boundaries of the Loop; and suburban trains were by 1885

Above, *"Illinois Central Station at Woodlawn, 1872" by James E. McBurney;* below, *along Lake Michigan, Illinois Central Railroad, 1865.*

running along their own separate main-line tracks and not on those which carried long-distance passengers or freight. This *was* the way to run a railroad.

The Illinois Central's early experience in the Hyde Park area was surely of some use in anticipating and meeting the needs of the growing number of commuters. Paul Cornell was a typically plain-spoken Chicago entrepreneur and had little difficulty in convincing the railroad's owners to back his real-estate venture. An advertisement for his community which appeared in the late 1850s is typical of the buoyancy and determination of this and other similar projects of the period:

> Hyde Park is beautifully situated on high ground interspersed with groves on the lake shore six miles from Chicago. The drives in the surrounding country are numerous and varied by picturesque groves. A special train leaves the Illinois

Central depot at intervals during the day . . . to accommodate residents. The trip is a delightful one all along the lake shore. As the population increases this will no doubt be a flag stop for every train coming on this road to Chicago.

It was to be much more than a flag stop. By 1871 there were twenty trains daily and service had been extended to 71st Street. Hyde Park, it was said at the time, "combines to a degree only rivaled by Evanston the delights of *rus in urbe*." In 1900 there were 114 weekday trains serving Hyde Park and nearby Woodlawn.

Riders today on the Illinois Central will have some difficulty in recognizing the route described by Cornell. There is now nothing attractive about the burned-out district between the Loop and 47th Street, although with a little effort one will discover that portions of Prairie Avenue and adjoining blocks have been resurrected in recent years. Once the most fashionable neighborhood in all of Chicago—the home of the Armours, the Fields, and the site of H.H. Richardson's architectural masterpiece, Glessner House—it is slowly being given back a bit of its former glory. Surviving mansions and town houses of Kenwood and Hyde Park have found new owners in the multiracial professional class that has long looked to the University of Chicago for its cultural direction and education.

The majority of today's commuters are headed further south—to apartments in the South Shore neighborhood or to one-family homes in the middle-class area outside the city limits in such new towns as Park Forest and Olympia Fields. These thousands of riders probably couldn't care less about appearances so long as the trains run on time. The Illinois Central's record in this respect is better than that of any other despite the fact that the railroad is the last of the commuter lines to receive modern equipment. It has made do with creaky steel coaches equipped with wicker seats since the 1920s. Now the Illinois Central is tied in with the public Regional Transportation Authority, and modern cars have been introduced into service. There is every expectation that service will continue to improve from the lows reached in the post-World War II period.

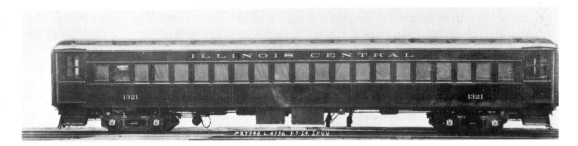

First lightweight suburban car built for the Illinois Central by Pullman Standard in 1924.

One price of modern-day progress has been the destruction of the railroad's central station at the south end of Grant Park. When built in 1893, it stood as a symbol of all that was comfortable and enlightened in free-enterprise railroading. In addition to this building complex, the Illinois Central also maintained conveniently-situated stations for its suburban passengers at Van Buren and Randolph Streets. The original main station stood at South Water Street. In the 1920s the railroad came to an agreement with the city to relinquish its lake shore riparian rights. With tracks depressed from view along this stretch from 12th Street to the Prudential Building, the dream of a city beautiful was finally realized.

Commuters on Chicago's other lines have long found the Illinois Central a strange phenomenon. It is the only one of the original steam railroads to have been electrified and, therefore, to have used MU (multiple-use) cars. The process of electrification should not have changed the image of the Illinois Central, but it did. Suburban service on the Lackawanna and Reading railroads, for instance, was not perceived as being that different when steam engines were replaced by the same kind of electromotive cars during the 1920s. The modern-era Illinois Central, however, was and continues to be seen as a transit line, something a little better than a streetcar or elevated line. Long-time residents of the city's south side and south suburban district know much better. Although the rapid transit lines parallel some of the railroad's routes (as does also the Chicago, South Shore & South Bend interurban), the Illinois Central tracks provide middle-class neighborhoods with much more convenient service. Under the direction of the Regional Transportation Authority, there certainly will be some changes in the name of efficiency, but it is to be hoped that well-established patterns of commuting and residential living will not be thrown away.

The Chicago, Burlington & Quincy Railroad

No railroad in the 20th century has so captured the imagination of the public as the Burlington. When the economic future of all business enterprise appeared dim in the 1930s, the Burlington's new trains of dynamic design and modern diesel power—the Zephyrs—struck just the right note of confidence. Ralph Budd, president of the railroad, is credited with successfully launching this revolution in long-distance passenger travel. He was truly a masterful railroadman and executive. The company he administered through the extremely difficult middle years of the 20th century had been built up over a 100-year period to respond to the ups and downs of the economic barometer. This flexibility was demonstrated in the earliest years of the railroad when commuter stations were arranged along the Aurora to Chicago main line and again in 1950 when the Burlington was the first Chicago-area carrier to introduce stainless-steel gallery cars to suburban service.

The Burlington began in 1849, not in the city, but in the country, in Aurora some thirty-eight miles southwest of Chicago. The Aurora Branch Railroad was completed through Batavia to the Galena's main line at West Chicago in 1850. For the next fourteen years, use was made of the North Western's early track to and from Chicago. During the same period the Aurora branch was restructured and enlarged to the southwest and emerged in 1855 as the Chicago, Burlington & Quincy. A state charter granted in 1854 allowed for the building of a straight or air-line route between Aurora and Chicago. Work was finally begun in 1862 under the direction of the company's president, John Van Nortwick, a resident of Batavia and a member of a family that would long be active in the affairs of that village and adjoining Geneva. By 1864 the independent line was finished. Although most of the Burlington's wealth was to be gained as a result of its preeminent position as a Middle-Western and Rocky-Mountain freight carrier, the railroad's roots in the small towns west of Chicago were not to be forgotten or neglected in the succeeding 100 years.

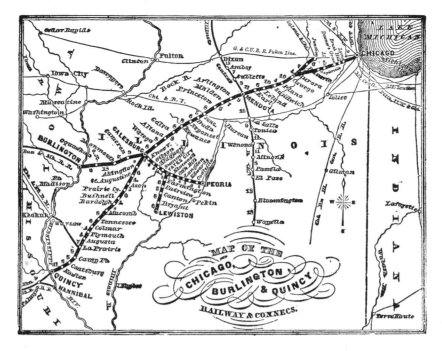

Chicago, Burlington & Quincy Railroad, 1866.

There were small settlements to serve between the city and Aurora, such stops on a stagecoach route as La Grange, Downers Grove, and Naperville. There was also the opportunity to establish new settlements along the tracks. At first the developers concentrated on the easternmost section, and they were aided and directed in their enterprise by the railroad. William Robbins, a St. Louis banker, bought 800 acres in 1864 and began to lay out the new village of Hinsdale alongside the earlier settlement of Fullersburg once he was sure the railroad would pass through the area. His grant of a right-of-way through the tract assured that trains would stop there. By the time the trains began arriving, Robbins was well ensconced in his own country manor, "Woodside." He is given credit for the name *Hinsdale*. Several reasons have been given for the choice, but the fact that H.W. Hinsdale of Chicago was one of the Burlington's directors probably had much to do with the decision. J.M. Walker, attorney for the line and later its president, acquired 370 acres south of the tracks in the Hinsdale-Clarendon Hills area and began their proper development. Hinsdale also became the home of A.T. Hall, treasurer of the railroad, and of Robert Harris, general superintendent and later president.

By the early '70s there were twenty-four daily trains to the city, and fares were affordable for even some middle-income families. A yearly commutation ticket cost $75; family tickets were available for 20¢ a ride. Fares were still not much higher on a mile basis than those charged at the time by streetcar companies serving the inner-city neighborhoods. With this kind of encouragement, it was only natural that—despite sporadic periods of economic depression—development should continue to boom along the Burlington. In 1872 Oliver J. Stough, a Chicago financier who had purchased 1,200 acres adjoining the tracks in Hinsdale and Clarendon Hills, began to lay out streets and to build model homes. He was joined in these ventures by Burlington executives Walker and Harris. Robbins, still active as a developer, commissioned landscape architect H.W.S. Cleveland to design a plan of gracefully curving tree-lined streets for his acreage. It was not long before Hinsdale gained the reputation among city businessmen as one of the most charming and socially desirable suburban towns.

Many of the homes were in the $8,000 to $15,000 class, mansions by today's values and standards. Like called unto like, and joining the Burlington executives and investors were such early residents as Charles E. Raymond, president of the First National Bank of Chicago, and Frank Osgood Butler, a papermaker and founding father of two Chicago-area institutions, Butler Industries and the Oak Brook Polo Club. "Millionaires' Row" of palatial homes along County Line Road (dividing DuPage and Cook Counties) became known throughout the country in the late 19th century and was the Midwest's version of the Madison Avenue procession of estates which ran through Madison, Florham Park, and Morristown, New Jersey.

The millionaires gave Hinsdale class; the upper middle class provided bourgeois respectability. As early as 1874 fifty homes costing between $1,500 and $2,000 each were being built on smaller lots to satisfy the needs of those who kept only one home and one horse—and that, not for sporting purposes, but for transportation. Two-thousand dollars would pay for a substantial home in those days, however, and it was likely to be a tasteful Victorian affair. Building lots were more than ample in space for a barn or stable, vegetable and flower gardens, and a proper drive. Unlike those in Evanston and other earlier villages, the enlightened developers chose to arrange streets in pleasant winding patterns that enhanced the beauty of the natural landscape. Public-spirited men, they also provided residents with handsome churches and school buildings and saw to it that architecturally-impressive stations—three in number for the area—were erected in convenient places.

In the early 20th century Hinsdale was about as comfortable and prosperous a suburban town as any in America. Fullersburg to the north was incorporated with the village in 1923. The town remains today an exceptionally quiet and well-tended garden spot. A guide to DuPage County first compiled in the 1930s by members of a Federal Writers' Project team of the Works Progress Administration presents an interesting look at the town. It is ironic that the observations—positive in tone—should come from writers representing a program loathed by a majority of Hinsdale residents who kept up with politics by reading the high-Republican *Chicago Tribune:*

> The Hinsdale of the Coolidge era was a world of splendid houses and physically impressive civic institutions, of women's clubs and bridge clubs, horseback riding and golf. It was a world built and maintained by brisk and prosperous bankers, manufacturers, brokers, realtors, junior executives, and insurance salesmen. Influential community leaders, recruited chiefly from the residents of Millionaires' Row prevented the rise of those speculative subdivisions with sidewalks, paved avenues, and street lights, but not inhabitants, which today in utter desuetude, give a dismal face to many an American town.

In the 1920s hundreds of thousands of acres of suburban land across the country had been laid out for development, and when the economy declined, many of these areas took on the appearance of ghost towns. Hinsdale wanted no part of it, and had the wealth and influence during the '20s to keep the latter-day speculators at bay. Following World War II, another great wave of development threatened the social structure of the town and this, too, was diverted in other directions—mainly to the west. The reasons for rejection may have been spurious, grounded as they were in privilege, but the underlying argument can only be appreciated. Why sacrifice well-planned, aesthetically designed space for the straight, cramped lines of get-rich-quick modern development?

Hinsdale was not alone in facing these problems. Riverside, several miles to the

Top, *Hinsdale (Illinois) Station, 1960s;* bottom, *Highlands Station, Hinsdale, Illinois, 1960s;*

northeast along the Burlington, had been laid out in the late 1860s as a model garden city. The Riverside Improvement Company made up of Chicago businessmen bought 1,600 acres in 1866, 700 of which were devoted to roads, borders, walks, recreational grounds, and parks. The New York architectural landscaping firm of Frederick Law Olmstead and Calvert Vaux was brought in to execute the design and they were immensely successful. Sixty-thousand shrubs and trees were planted in attractive sites along the winding Des Plaines River and the curving streets. "Riverside, before it passed into the hands of the Company," it was written in 1874,

Top, *awaiting the commuter train at Hinsdale Station, 1920s;* bottom, *Riverside (Illinois) Station, 1920s. Both, Chicago, Burlington & Quincy Railroad.*

"possessed many beautiful groves of trees—elm, maple, and oak; but it was left for the standing wooded land to be utilized to its utmost extent by the skill of the artist. Everything likely to give the place the appearance of a resident park was done." There were economic difficulties for the company to overcome in the '70s, but the constant increase in Chicago's population as it rebuilt after the Great Fire provided more than sufficient numbers of financially-qualified residents. It is said that the company eventually netted $7 million on its investment of $1.5 million. The town did not attract as many of Chicago's wealthiest families as did Hinsdale, but in most respects it was a more successful undertaking both for the investors and generations of fortunate residents. It stands today virtually alone in a sea of vast and intensive suburban development.

The Burlington moved rapidly after World War II to convert as many of the new suburbanites as possible to the advantages of train service. Statistically the railroad has been successful: The number of passengers from such towns as Clarendon Hills, Lisle, and La Grange Park rose more than 100 percent from 1950, when the new equipment was introduced, to 1960. Progress since that time has been impressive despite the opening of the East-West Tollway to Aurora from Chicago. Now with the decline of gasoline supplies an acknowledged fact, the railroad should boom as never before. Suburban service is tied in with the public Regional Transportation Authority, and all equipment has been sold to that agency. The Burlington, merged with the Northern Pacific, remains, however, a vigorous carrier of freight, and its Zephyrs continue to serve the West as part of the Amtrak inter-city passenger system.

Service beyond the Hinsdale-Clarendon Hills area has been increased in recent years as more and more towns have attracted residential development. For many years Downers Grove was the terminus for one-half the suburban runs, the others continuing on to Aurora. Since 1952 Aurora has been the end of the line for all trains. This has meant much more convenient rush-hour service for Lisle, Naperville, and parts of Aurora. Unfortunately, the railroad was not able to take as great a direct hand in the linking of new developments with their line as had been the case in the 19th century. Branch lines were not established in the 1900s to serve the new residents of villages away from the main line. If the Burlington had attempted such projects at an earlier date when their need was less apparent, the cost might have proved a serious drain on the company's financial resources. Consequently, unlike many Eastern railroads, the Burlington has never had to cut back significantly on its service.

The Chicago & North Western Railway

What the New York Central was to New Yorkers and the Pennsylvania to Philadelphians, the North Western was to Chicagoans—the best. Its oldest railroad, the North Western became also Chicago's richest and largest. During the Gilded Age suburban gentlemen from the North Shore could travel in private subscription cars which were every bit the equal of those to be found in the East; less fortunate commuters were at least assured of convenient service to any one of several hundred suburban neighborhoods. The North Western was more than a railroad line; it was a "system" called in the 1870s "the only railroad which Chicago, with her hundred passenger trains a day, her palatial depots, and her acknowledged character as the pivot of the national railway system, ever really evolved." Service on three suburban divisions—the Galena directly west, the Wisconsin to the northwest, and the Milwaukee due north—was in existence by 1870. Lake View on the north side of Chicago and Evanston had been provided with rush-hour trains earlier, but there was not a great demand for special service and rates until after the Civil War. In 1864 the name *Chicago & North Western Railway* emerged as a result of the merger of several different lines with the pioneer Galena & Chicago Union Railway, which had been chartered in 1836 but not completed between these two towns until after 1850. The 1864 consolidation gave the new North Western everything it needed to become not only a premier freight carrier but also Chicago's leading passenger line.

With the exception of the south-side Hyde Park development, the first significant suburban movement was to the north along the lake shore. Following the Great Fire of 1871 which leveled much more of the city's north side than the south, the movement north of Fullerton Avenue into Lake View was extremely rapid. The

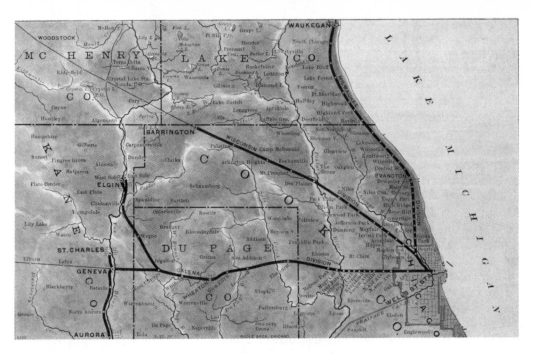

Suburban district, Chicago & North Western Railway, 1900.

Chicago & Milwaukee Railway, taken over by the North Western, provided the means for escape from the congested city core. By 1874 the Lake View area was described as "thickly settled," but there was plenty of room to be had in adjoining Ravenswood which had been laid out in 1869 by a land improvement company. There were then fourteen daily trains that made the trip between the city and the northern villages in roughly twenty minutes. The railroad encouraged settlement with a fare that amounted to no more than a penny for each of the eight to ten miles to be traversed. Rogers Park, a few more miles farther on, was just in the process of being settled in 1874, but five trains already stopped there each day.

The peaceful village of Evanston provided the model for the northern expansion. First settled in the 1830s, it was a sober-sided, respectable enclave of Methodist learning. Even its streets, as a commentator in the 1870s put it, "run at right angles and show no suspicion of a curve either to the right or left . . . . Evanston bears the stamp of its devoutly-inclined founders. Its garb is cut as squarely as though it were 'of the cloth' and its morals are as strict as those of a New England village." Many of the new suburban villages indulged the fancy of gently curving streets and roads, but not Evanston. By the end of the century, when Chicago's northern city line defined Evanston's southern boundary, the town was just as straight-laced and Protestant. Naturally, the Women's Christian Temperance Union and its founder, Frances Willard, found Evanston a congenial place to call home.

Teetotaling was also practiced in other northern suburban towns that modeled themselves on Evanston, except for its grid pattern. Winnetka, incorporated in 1869, was a dry town—at the time. And so was Highland Park where a building association guided the sale of land and its proper use. Lake Forest presents a somewhat different story—not that it was wet, just more sophisticated and wealthy. The village had been founded in 1856 by an association of Chicago Presbyterian church members. Two-thousand acres were purchased, and, of these, sixty-two were set aside for a respectable seat of higher learning. Thus was born Lake Forest Academy, a boy's preparatory school, and then Ferry Hall for girls, and later, Lake

Views of Kenilworth, Illinois; Chicago & North Western Railway station at lower left, 1900.

Forest College. Barat College, a Sacred Heart institution, was a much later development. In the 1870s the town was termed "the favorite resort of the better class of Chicago's inhabitants." Twenty-eight miles from Chicago, it did serve admirably as a summer retreat for many families. An elegant hotel overlooked the lake. Thanks to the North Western, residents of Lake Forest could easily enjoy their proper village "and at the same time pursue their active business life in the city." The trip took only an hour and fifteen minutes in 1866, and three trains ran in each direction daily.

Development to the west of Chicago proceeded along the lines of the North Western's original route established by the Galena & Chicago Union. Austin and Oak Park were two of the earliest bedroom communities. The former, founded by a prosperous city merchant of the same name, was eventually made a part of the city, but Oak Park (earlier known as Oak Ridge, Harlem, or Noyesville) remained independent—fiercely so. While Evanston was predominantly Methodist and Lake Forest Presbyterian, Oak Park was Congregationalist of the most true-blue New England variety. It was founded, as were the other towns, at a time when one's membership in a religious denomination greatly determined how nonworking hours were spent. Although there was no college, education of the finest sort was

Lake Forest (Illinois) Station, Chicago & North Western Railway, 1970s.

Views of Elmhurst, Illinois; Chicago & North Western Railway station at upper right, 1900.

stressed in local literature of the time as being of paramount importance. The town was termed in the 1870s the "favorite resort for literary and religious people." Frank Lloyd Wright was to design some of his most successful homes for Oak Park residents, and here, too, that most American of literary figures, Ernest Hemingway, spent his youth. It was not the kind of town that Vachel Lindsay or Mark Twain would have found congenial.

Other western suburban towns followed the lead of Oak Park after the Civil War—Elmhurst (originally called Cottage Hill), and Lombard (formerly Babcock's Grove) were two typical villages which grew from a handful of people in the 1870s to over 500 in twenty years. Just beyond on the North Western was Glen Ellyn, first known as Danby and then Prospect Park. It developed as a summer resort, with a lake within the village and a fine hotel. The local spring water was prized for its purity, and many who drank of it decided that the locale was a good place for permanent settlement. Twenty-three miles west of the city, it could be reached by rail in less than an hour's time.

Farther west from the city was the DuPage County seat of Wheaton, the North Western's junction point with the Burlington at West Chicago, and the neat Fox River Valley towns of Elgin, St. Charles, Geneva, Batavia, and Aurora. Each had been founded by New Englanders of an industrious sort, and each desired some part of the emerging rail transportation system. Elgin was reached by the old Galena line in 1850; Aurora acquired its own railroad, the Burlington, the same year; and the Burlington also passed through Batavia. St. Charles pushed through its own branch line to the Galena in 1849, and until 1853 a few Genevans may have made their way to the city via this route. In this year the Galena-backed Chicago, Dixon & Iowa Air-Line was completed from the junction at West Chicago to Geneva and in 1854 reached Dixon. When the consolidation of lines resulted in the emergence of the North Western system, it was the Dixon route which was chosen as the main line to the West rather than the old route via Elgin. Geneva slowly developed as a commuting town after the Civil War and was the home for some of the North Western's executives, among them one man, Joel Harvey, who managed the North Western's successful development of industrial land closer to the city during the 1870s. By the turn of the century it had become the last stop on the Galena suburban division.

Perhaps because of Geneva's central geographic position and its selection as the Kane County seat, it was destined to become—in proportion to its population—the chief Fox Valley commuting town. The transportation link to the city was taken advantage of to encourage the growth of cultural institutions and to attract residents who would make the town a respected one. By the 1890s the railroad made it possible to attend the opera, symphony, and theater in Chicago on any night of the week except Sunday. The so-called "opera train" made its return trip at 11:40 p.m. In this respect, Geneva was by no means unique; it was merely more fortunate. Although only an hour away from the city by train, it was thirty-five miles distant, and, in the timetable of suburban development, that allowed more than enough time to set down unwritten rules of social behavior and the institutions with which to encourage their practice.

The residents of the towns along the North Western's third suburban division, the Wisconsin, were undoubtedly just as concerned in the 1880s and '90s about the proper development of village life. Through acquisition in 1864 of the Chicago, St. Anthony & Fond du Lac Railway, the North Western gained access to Irving Park, Norwood Park, Des Plaines, Arlington Heights, and Barrington. The first two villages were among six served by the railroad which were eventually annexed by the city. In 1900 the North Western called these settlements "inner-city suburbs" which "combine the advantages of suburban life with the public conveniences of this great city." In a brochure entitled "The Beautiful Country Near Chicago," the passenger department insisted that such inner-city spots "retain, however, the beauty of spacious grounds and pretty homes." Undoubtedly, the residents of Arlington Heights, originally called Dunton, disagreed in the 1890s. Theirs was still an area fit for a country gentleman with room enough for fine orchards and the training of horses. Subdivision had begun as early as the 1870s. At the same time the town fathers—all with large investments in land—saw to it that sufficient space was allowed for public amenities in the village center. The depot was a handsome structure and was attractively landscaped. The grounds comprised twenty acres and these were, according to a contemporary account, "laid out and fenced off into romantic parks, ornamented with shade, evergreen trees, and shrubbery in great variety." What better sight to greet the prospective home owner or the weary businessman returning from the city at the end of a hard day?

All of the railroad's suburban divisions prospered during the first two decades of the 1900s. The towns closest to the city were, of course, the first to slip in the esteem of the trendsetters in high society and in the real-estate trade. Oak Park was

A row of fashionable Queen Anne residences, Barrington, Illinois, 1900.

Passenger car built by the Standard Steel Car Co. for the Chicago & North Western Railway.

abandoned by some for Geneva; Evanston for Winnetka; Des Plaines for Arlington Heights or Barrington. As elsewhere in the country, the pace of residential development increased tremendously after World War I and was only slowed down to a crawl by the stock market crash and the ensuing Depression. In 1929 the North Western carried as many passengers as it would again for another forty years. Its equipment, all-steel passenger cars and powerful steam locomotives, were as up-to-date as any used in the country. But from then on—until the arrival of new management in the early 1950s—it was all downhill.

Today there are over 100,000 daily passengers who travel in bi-level gallery cars of considerable riding comfort and design appeal. Steam engines were banned in 1956. Except for a few commuter club cars and other older pieces of equipment, all the railroad's rolling stock has been sold to the Regional Transportation Authority. The great yellow and green streamliners headed for Portland, Seattle, Denver, San Francisco, and Los Angeles no longer streak westward along the suburban main line to meet the Union Pacific at Omaha. The North Western name, however, has not been sold nor has the company subsided into the bankrupt state reached by a majority of Eastern and Midwestern lines. The railroad has been around too long for it to lose all of its character overnight to an anonymous public agency.

A Chicago & North Western Railway bi-level train at the Glencoe stop en route to Chicago, 1959.

The Chicago, Milwaukee, St. Paul & Pacific Railroad

A railroad established in Wisconsin in 1864, the Milwaukee Road did not enter the adjacent Illinois territory until the 1870s. Passengers traveling the Chicago to Milwaukee route before that time could easily pass over the North Western tracks which paralleled Lake Michigan. The North Western also provided good service to such south-central Wisconsin towns as Janesville, Beloit, Madison, and Watertown on a branch line or the Wisconsin division from Chicago. Why, then, should the Milwaukee Road—formally known as the Chicago, Milwaukee, St. Paul & Pacific— build a line from the Wisconsin border to Chicago in 1872? The answer is simple—a desire to capture as much of the booming freight and passenger business between the two areas as was possible. By the 1870s, Chicago had emerged as the preeminent rail center, the gate through which one passed to reach the East or the West. Eventually the main offices of the Milwaukee Road were moved from Wisconsin to Chicago. There really was no choice if the railroad was to realize its ambitions as a major rail carrier.

Between 1872 and 1900 business increased greatly. Their lease in 1880 of the Chicago & Pacific Railroad's line to Elgin and westward provided a more direct link to Omaha, Kansas City, and Denver than had an earlier connection from Milwaukee. Very slowly but surely the Milwaukee Road became involved in the suburban commuter business on both the West line to Elgin and the North line along its route to Milwaukee. The latter line paralleled the North Western's North Shore route. A third suburban route, a branch line, was opened as far as Calvary on the southern border of Evanston in 1885 and extended as far as Wilmette in 1888. The time was late to start in the commuter business, and the areas through which the Milwaukee Road passed were only sparsely settled in the late 19th century. Until a half-century later, vast portions of the territory reached by the Elgin or West line remained without large-scale development.

The Milwaukee Road seemed to have a good thing going for it in the Evanston branch line. Its need was recognized as early as 1874. At that time a booster of the town explained that "When the Chicago, Milwaukee & St. Paul Railroad shall put in a branch to the town, . . . real estate owners on the west side look for a day of harvest that shall surpass the most sanguine expectations." The population of the west side, he explained, was almost equal to that of the east served by the North Western. By the 1890s there were as many as ten daily Milwaukee Road trains to Evanston and eleven others which continued on to Wilmette. Revenue from the passengers, however, never began to meet the cost of service. Perhaps growth just didn't come fast enough to satisfy the railroad. Whatever the reason, service was drastically reduced by 1905, and the line was leased two years later to the North Western Elevated Railroad Co. from Graceland Avenue to Linden Avenue, Wilmette. Later the Chicago, North Shore & Milwaukee, an electric interurban, was also granted use of the line. During World War I the tracks were elevated through the city, and eventually the branch was sold to the Chicago Transportation Authority.

It would not have been surprising if the railroad had not also sought to cut back its service on the West and North lines during the same period, but the story was just the opposite. Frequency of trains was increased, albeit slowly, and the suburban

Above, *restored station, Deerfield, Illinois, 1976;* below, *new station, Morton Grove, Illinois, 1976.* *Both, Milwaukee Road.*

territory was expanded. A branch to Libertyville from Roundout on the North line had been completed in 1881, and over the next twenty years was extended as far as Janesville, Wisconsin. Most of the riders on the North line were from such towns as Morton Grove, Glenview, Northbrook, and Deerfield. The region beyond was a vacation land of quiet lakes and cottages and, although much more developed today, remains a distinct country district. The Morton Grove to Roundout section was probably somewhat similar in the 1890s and early 1900s. The villages were tiny by comparison with those farther east along the lake. The whole area was suitable for city residents seeking an expansive spread rather than a subdivided plot of land. Out on the Libertyville branch, the opportunities for gentleman farmers were even greater. Here there was plenty of room to breed horses and cattle. There was little room or tolerance for vast numbers of such creatures in Lake Forest or Winnetka.

At the same time that the Milwaukee Road was expanding its service to country gentlemen, it was continuing to serve city dwellers living in the suburban neighborhoods of Chicago. On the North line the Grayland and Montrose areas were especially favored. The Grayland subdivision was located between Irving Park and Montrose Boulevards and had been founded by farmer John Gray in 1873. Despite competition from the North Western's Wisconsin division, the Milwaukee Road, it was reported at the time, decided "to put on suburban trains which will make at least four trips a day. This railroad corporation has spared no expense in perfecting the road . . . . The rolling stock is all new and first class in every respect." Montrose lay to the north, and was also served by both railroads. Like Grayland, it was already thickly settled.

Service on the West line to Elgin was largely restricted in the early years to villages since annexed to the city or found close by today. Humboldt, Galewood, and Mont Clare were three of the first suburban favorites. As the name indicates, Humboldt was established by an association of German businessmen. When

Arriving at the old Itasca (Illinois) Station, on the West line, Milwaukee Road, 1976.

founded in 1872, half the development was situated just outside the city limits at Division Street. Galewood was settled at the same time that the railroad was established, and the Milwaukee Road owned half of the tract of 320 acres. For a time there was a busy branch line north from here to the village of Dunning. Mont Clare, four-tenths of a mile beyond, originally included 178 acres and was extensively subdivided in the 1870s and '80s. There was never more than a handful of trains serving these towns each day, and the schedule included only three or four which made the complete run as far as Elgin. River Grove, or River Park as it was originally called, was about as long a trip as most travelers on the Milwaukee road wanted to make in the late 1800s. This was and is still a particularly beautiful area lying along the Des Plaines River, and, although it was not developed with the same care as Riverside, much attention was given to the natural landscape. The railroad station was itself located in a five-acre public park.

It is rare to find a commuter railroad that has dramatically increased its service since the 1920s, but the Milwaukee Road is one of them, at least since World War II on the West line. There are now twenty-one trains serving the area and, with proper public funding, the number will continue to grow. Elgin was one of the cities first served by the North Western, but not even the oldest resident can remember when the trains of this company supplied much more than freight. Since the early 1950s, the whole northwestern stretch from Bensenville and O'Hare International Airport to Elgin—passing through Itasca, Roselle, Hanover Park, and Bartlett along the way—has boomed unlike any other in the Chicago area. The Milwaukee Road was not in the best condition to handle the expansion, but it managed throughout the 1950s to retire its steam locomotives and to freshen up its old steel passenger coaches. Further improvements came in the '60s with the modification of a few long-distance Hiawatha streamliner cars for suburban use and the addition of new bi-level coaches in 1961 and '65. The Milwaukee Road has since sold all of its suburban fleet to the Regional Transportation Authority, and has received from them in turn even newer coaches. Public funds are also being used for the rehabilitation or building of new stations. In 1977 there were approximately 16,000 daily riders on the two lines; today there are at least 19,000.

The Chicago, Rock Island & Pacific Railroad

The Rock Island line—famed in song and story—has never been a particularly romantic feature of the Chicago railroading scene, but it has played an important role in the growth of the city and its southwestern suburbs reaching as far as Joliet. The easternmost section of the line was completed in 1852, and the main line, reaching as far west as Rock Island on the Mississippi River, was in full operation by 1854. At this time Chicago proper extended only to 39th Street; beyond this boundary along the Rock Island lay such communities as Englewood and South Englewood. Naturally, they were to develop as early commuting neighborhoods. Englewood, also known as Junction, was well-situated to receive city dwellers, and a choice could be made there between the Rock Island or two other railroads—the Lake Shore & Michigan Southern (later absorbed into the New York Central

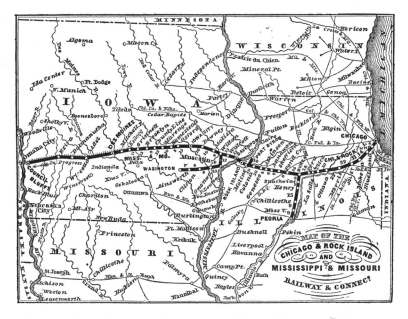

Chicago, Rock Island & Mississippi & Misouri Railway, 1866.

system) and the Pittsburgh, Fort Wayne & Chicago (leased to the Pennsylvania in 1869)—which also carried passengers to and from the city from the 1860s on. In 1874 there were twenty-eight trains serving the locality of some 3,000 people. The town was then considered to be fully settled and was in the process of forming its own "suburbs" to the southwest. There was an especially attractive six-mile-long region between 89th Street and Blue Island known as the Blue Island ridge, and it was here that the Rock Island would earn its reputation as a useful and efficient carrier of suburban traffic.

Three miles south of Englewood came South Englewood, and beyond the village lay what was then called Washington Heights along the six-mile Blue Island ridge. The Blue Island Land and Building Co. began plotting out lots in several areas of the Heights, including those which now comprise the Morgan Park and Beverly Hills neighborhoods of Chicago. Real-estate activity was so feverish in the early '70s that the Rock Island constructed a special branch which left the main line at 99th Street and reentered it at the village of Blue Island. Officials of the railroad were

South Englewood (Chicago) Depot, Chicago, Rock Island & Pacific Railroad, 1874.

among those active in the land company and stood to profit enormously from the successful execution of the real-estate scheme. The success achieved was beyond anyone's hopes; in 1872 $267,743 worth of lots were purchased, and these were only a fraction of the total of 1,500 acres bought by the company for $150,000 in 1869. Sale of the land to home owners was made easier by the liberal terms offered by the well-capitalized company. It built the houses and then made them available on a time-payment basis. The intention, according to a contemporary report, was to "enable people of moderate means to secure a home, and avoid the payment of high rents in the city."

One of the most appealing of the Washington Heights subdivisions was Morgan Park. Land, averaging $20 per foot in the early '70s, was considerably more expensive than elsewhere in the area. Morgan Park was to serve as a drawing card for the "better sort." A military academy for boys, originally called the Mt. Vernon Military and Classical Academy, was built on a site donated by the land company and provided a cultural base for the community. It exists today as the Morgan Park Military Academy. The Rock Island made certain, of course, that commutation rates encouraged settlement. In case there was any hesitation about settling down twelve miles from the city, arrangements were made by the subdivision's owners for the railroad to charge new residents only 10¢ a ride for the first two years of residence. There were 187 residents of the village in 1880, and by 1890 it had grown to over a thousand. In the preceding year the Rock Island lengthened the branch line by two-and-a-half miles to better serve the area. Not until 1914 would Morgan Park become part of the city.

In the early 1900s the whole Rock Island territory was well settled as far as Blue Island, and the march toward Joliet, twenty-four miles farther on, was underway. Bremen (later known as Tinley Park), Mokena, and New Lenox were on the route of development. In 1907 the railroad's accounting department formally extended the boundaries of the suburban territory from Blue Island to Joliet. "Accommodation" trains had run from the small city of Joliet to Chicago for some years, but in the 20th century more were needed. The "Banker's Special" express was one answer. The Rock Island had long prided itself on its forty-five-minute service to Blue Island; the extra twenty-four miles to Joliet required only a half-hour more. Between World War I and 1929, both revenue and the number of passengers carried on the line doubled. Then came the Depression.

The Rock Island fared no better than most other commuter lines. For years it had been unable to establish reasonable rates for commutation. Having set the precedent of heavily subsidizing suburban travel in order to sell land, it was difficult for the company's executives to turn around and ask for more money from the riders. When they tried, they were often blocked by the state regulators. In the late 1940s the Rock Island spent five-million dollars which it did not have on modernizing passenger car equipment. Since that time everything possible has been done to further improve service; the old Standard Steel cars from the 1920s and Pullman-Standard coaches dating to 1949 have been replaced by seventy-five bi-levels, half of which are owned by the Regional Transportation Authority. Ridership has been increasing at a rate of seven to eight percent over the past few years, and the rate is likely to accelerate in the future as more and more commuters abandon their cars.

Illustration Credits

Color illustrations (in order of appearance): Courtesy, Chase Manhattan Bank Collection; private collection; Picture Collection, New York Public Library; Peter Ferencze, photographer; Ibid; The New-York Historical Society; Picture Collection, New York Public Library; The New-York Historical Society; Courtesy, Avery Library, Columbia University; Ibid; Smithsonian Institution, Museum of History and Technology; Ranulph Bye; Ibid; Ibid; Courtesy, Norton D. Clark; Ibid; Library of Congress; Ibid; Ibid; Ibid; Smithsonian Institution, Museum of History and Technology.

Black and white illustrations (in order of appearance):

Frontispiece: Library of Congress, John Collier, photographer. Part I: "The Beautiful Country Near Chicago," Chicago & North Western Railway; Geneva, Illinois, Public Library District; Smithsonian Institution, Museum of History and Technology; Ibid. Part II: Picture Collection, New York Public Library; Library of Congress; *The American Railway.* Part III: Picture Collection, New York Public Library; Smithsonian Institution, Museum of History and Technology; private collection; Smithsonian Institution, Museum of History and Technology; Part IV: Smithsonian Institution, Museum of History and Technology; *The American Railway;* Library of Congress; Association of American Railroads; Library of Congress; Association of American Railroads; Library of Congress; Picture Collection, New York Public Library; Ibid.

New York: Library of Congress; *The American Railway;* Picture Collection New York Public Library; private collection. New York Central: Private collection; Ibid; Picture Collection, New York Public Library; private collection; Smithsonian Institution, Museum of History and Technology; private collection; Museum of the City of New York, J. Clarence Davies Collection; *Buildings & Structures of American Railroads;* private collection; New York Central; William B. May Co.; *ABC Pathfinder Railway Guide;* private collection; Picture Collection, New York Public Library; *Buildings & Structures of American Railroads;* private collection; Library of Congress, Dorothea Lange, photographer; Library of Congress. New York, New Haven & Hartford: *ABC Pathfinder Railway Guide; Buildings & Structures of American Railroads;* private collection; Smithsonian Institution, Museum of History and Technology; Library of Congress; Ibid. Long Island Railroad: Private collection; Brooklyn Public Library, Brooklyn Collection, George Brainard Collection; Ibid; private collection; Library of Congress; Ibid; Picture Collection, New York Public Library. Delaware, Lackawanna & Western: Private collection; Library of Congress; private collection; Courtesy, Thomas T. Taber III; Ibid; Library of Congress; Courtesy, Thomas T. Taber III; Library of Congress. Erie Railroad: Private collection; Historic American Engineering Record; Ibid; Ibid; private collection; Library of Congress; Ibid. Central Railroad of New Jersey: Private collection; *The Central Railroad of New Jersey;* Ibid; Historic American Engineering Record, Jack E. Boucher, photographer; Smithsonian

Institution, Museum of History and Technology; private collection; Ibid; Ibid. **Pennsylvania Railroad:** Private collection; Ibid; Ibid; Railway & Locomotive Historical Society; private collection; Princeton University Archives; Ibid.

Philadelphia: Association of American Railroads. **Reading Lines:** Association of American Railroads; Courtesy, George M. Hart; Ibid; private collection; *Buildings & Structures of American Railroads;* private collection; *Buildings & Structures of American Railroads.* **Pennsylvania Railroad:** SEPTA; Historic American Buildings Survey, Jack E. Boucher, photographer; *Buildings & Structures of American Railroads;* SEPTA; Picture Collection, New York Public Library.

Boston: Private collection. **Boston & Albany:** *ABC Pathfinder Railway Guide;* Courtesy, Norton D. Clark; Ibid; Picture Collection, New York Public Library; Historic American Buildings Survey, Cervin Robinson; Railway & Locomotive Historical Society. **New York, New Haven & Hartford:** Private collection; Courtesy, Norton D. Clark; private collection; *ABC Pathfinder Railway Guide;* Railway & Locomotive Historical Society; Ibid; Ibid; *The American Railway;* Railway & Locomotive Historical Society. **Boston & Maine:** *ABC Pathfinder Railway Guide; The Engineering & Building Record;* Courtesy, Norton D. Clark, Ibid; Ibid, Ibid, Bill Ryerson, photographer; Railway & Locomotive Historical Society.

Chicago: Association of American Railroads. **Illinois Central:** Association of American Railroads; Ibid; Ibid. **Chicago, Burlington & Quincy:** Private Collection; Chicago, Burlington & Quincy Railroad; Ibid; Hinsdale, Illinois, Library; Chicago, Burlington & Quincy Railroad. **Chicago & North Western:** "The Beautiful Country Near Chicago," Chicago & North Western Railway; Ibid; Chicago & North Western Transportation Co.; "The Beautiful Country Near Chicago"; Ibid; Smithsonian Institution, Museum of History and Technology; Chicago & North Western Railroad. **Milwaukee Road:** Milwaukee Road, Tom Phillips, photographer; Ibid, Jim Scribbins, photographer; Ibid. **Chicago, Rock Island & Pacific:** Private collection; Ibid.

174

Index